Introduction

The Bailout Babies

Ireland is a country that punches above its weight.

The country has, in the past few years alone, had the fastest growing economy in the European Union. It has racked up billions of euro in budget surpluses. It has an out-sized influence on global affairs. And in the past four years it has been home to the world's most profitable Krispy Kreme doughnut shop, the world's busiest Domino's Pizza and the world's highest-earning IKEA outlet.

What a time to be Irish.

But while every generation has faced its own set of challenges – whether it's a lack of economic opportunity, a repressed social outlook or crushing levels of personal debt – there's something particularly cruel about the situation facing the young adults of today. Born into an era when anything seemed to be possible, the children of the Celtic Tiger undoubtedly had the greatest start of any generation in Ireland's history – on paper, at least. But – before they reached an age when they could take advantage of that – the rug was pulled, the door was shut, the tiger was shot.

So, who exactly am I talking about?

Any attempt to define a large group of a population is always going to be an inexact science. The best-known examples in popular culture today are the likes of the Boomers, Millennials and Gen Z – but these are crude (and often very US-centric) ideas. After all, the 'Boomers' got their name from America's post-Second World War baby boom. Ireland's population may also have been booming in the 1940s and 1950s – but it was less to do with a post-war euphoria and more down to the Catholic Church's 'go forth and multiply' approach to demographics.

Even 'Millennial' is a clumsy category. Sure, it hinges on a moment in time that all of us Gregorian-calendar stans experienced, but there's not much that an elder Millennial (born in the early 1980s) has in common with their younger (born in the mid-to-late 1990s) brethren. After all, one end of that spectrum is old enough to have been legally drinking pints when pubs still had to shut for the Sunday 'holy hour'. At the same time, those on the other end of the same span would have just been starting primary school. An elder Millennial likely earned their first wages in punt; the young Millennial probably couldn't even tell you which coin had the horse on it.

And, while the world may be getting smaller, does an American Millennial really have much of a shared experience with an Irish one? The truth is that these broad, international attempts to categorise generations don't carry much value – beyond giving us all an easy term to reach for when we want to sneer at people who aren't us.

But that's not to say that there are no ways to group together people within a certain age bracket – there are occasionally moments in time that represent a common bond for a group of people. And, in Ireland, the Celtic Tiger is one such moment.

It was a generation-defining event that, despite being relatively recent, is now etched deeply into the Irish psyche. And it is ground zero for so many of our current challenges.

In 1994, economist Kevin Gardiner wrote a report that tried to make sense of Ireland's remarkable economic situation. The country had been enjoying strong growth from the late 1980s onwards – becoming the fastest growing state in western Europe – but had somehow done so while dodging any domestic

The
Bailout
Babies

Adam Maguire is an award-winning TV, online and radio journalist working for Ireland's national broadcaster, RTÉ. He is focused on business, tech, media and current affairs. This is his first book.

The Bailout Babies

How Ireland's financial crash
reshaped the next generation –
and what it means for the future

Adam Maguire

Gill Books

Gill Books
Hume Avenue
Park West
Dublin 12
www.gillbooks.ie

Gill Books is an imprint of M.H. Gill and Co.

9781804583616

Design origination by Padraig McCormack
Edited by Heidi Houlihan
Proofread by Emma Dunne
Printed and bound in Great Britain by Clays Ltd, Elcograf S.p.A.
This book is typeset in 12pt on 16pt, Adobe Garamond Pro by Typo•glyphix

*The paper used in this book comes from the
wood pulp of sustainably managed forests.*

*To the best of our knowledge, this book complies in full with the requirements
of the General Product Safety Regulation (GPSR). For further information
and help with any safety queries, please contact us at productsafety@gill.ie.*

A CIP catalogue record for this book is available from the British Library.

5 4 3 2 1

To Sarah, who makes everything possible.

overheating. That was a near impossible task – and it was one the financial world had taken note of. He titled the report 'The Irish Economy: A Celtic Tiger', coining a term that instantly became a point of pride for policymakers (before, eventually, transforming into a jibe). But as miraculous as Ireland's growth had seemed to Gardiner as he wrote his paper, it was nothing compared to what happened next.

In 1994 itself, Irish gross domestic product (GDP) grew by 5.9 per cent (compared to 2.3 per cent in 1993). It hit 9.6 per cent in 1995, and climbed to 10.7 per cent in 1997, before bouncing around the 5–10 per cent range into the new millennium and beyond. That pace of expansion was so blistering that the 3 per cent rate recorded in 2003 (a rate that any other developed country would kill for) seemed disastrous to some.

At the same time unemployment nosedived, so much so that the country was in 'full' employment for all of the first half of the new decade. Meanwhile government debt tumbled as tax revenue funded motorways, trams, bridges and gargantuan symbolic spires – all while paying down the national credit card.

And while it might not be quite accurate to say that 'we all partied', most people benefitted in one way or another. That included a curious cohort of people – those born between 1990 and 2007 – officially the last cubs of the Celtic Tiger. When they entered the world – and possibly primary, and even secondary school – they were surrounded with what would have seemed like endless opportunities. KVI lunches and trips to Mosney were an alien concept to them. Instead, it was branded chocolate bars and sun holidays all the way. They grew up with the assumption that if they wanted anything – from a good job to a high-spec car – it would be there for the taking. And they knew that once they entered the real world, they'd only have to look in the general direction of a bank to get a mortgage for their own home (110 per cent, so they didn't have to hang around to buy that crushed velvet couch).

But by the time they were assessing their college and career options, the outlook had become very different. Opportunities were suddenly hard to come by. Holidays were luxuries once again. A mortgage was a pipe dream. Because, of course, all good things come to an end. Or, in this case, all speculation-and-reckless-lending-driven things come to an end.

In 2008, the country's economy contracted sharply, and the decline only deepened into 2009. Unemployment spiked, the banks faltered and the government borrowed heavily in an attempt to keep the country afloat. In the end, they opted to bring in outside assistance – the dreaded Troika – to help steady the ship. The resulting bailout is itself a landmark moment in Irish history. The country that emerged after the crash is not the same place it was before. And it's arguably those latter-stage Celtic Tiger Cubs who have carried the biggest burden from that moment.

These Bailout Babies – now aged from their late teens to their mid-30s – would have been too young to benefit from the rock-bottom house prices after the crash – but they would have felt the strain of the austerity that came with that. Assuming they didn't emigrate, they would have been entering the real world at a time when the economy was recovering – and recovering well. But the scars of the crash meant that the pay they could secure, and what the banks would let you do with that, was still austere.

Following an extended fallow period the building trade eventually returned to life, but until recently, developers were all too busy crafting high-spec office blocks for tech giants to think about lowly housing. That means the gap between demand and supply has only grown. At the same time, the once generous banks have become far more risk-averse, raising the financial bar for those who do manage to find a property within their budget. So getting a place of your own has quickly become an expensive endeavour once again – with prices only going one way.

That is where the Bailout Babies find themselves today – young adults who are victims of an economic situation that their parents and grandparents created. But it's not news that there is a housing crisis. In 2018, then Taoiseach Leo Varadkar declared it – and the homelessness it was contributing to – a national emergency. And the solutions, theories, claims and counter-claims are well worn at this stage.

But while that debate drags on, the Bailout Babies are trapped in its crossfire. And that doesn't just mean they can't afford a home of their own – the problems the situation has created bleed into every aspect of their lives. Meanwhile the future has become increasingly uncertain, with artificial intelligence (AI) threatening to destroy careers, and war and climate change threatening to destroy the planet.

But even though they may be victims of someone else's mistakes, the Bailout Babies aren't allowing themselves to be shackled by it. It's not like they are sitting their parents' box rooms waiting for the problem to be solved. Instead, having endured the Covid-19 pandemic, a second economic and social cataclysm in their short lives, they have become emboldened to seek out opportunities and determined to shape their own futures. They have become a force to be reckoned with. This generation are working hard to earn money – often good money. They are an ever-growing economic power in their own right, representing more than a quarter of the country's adult population. Most are finding new ways to keep going all while they hold out hope for something better. Many are showing remarkable creativity and hustle in their attempts to find a way around their financial bind. Others are opting to find meaning in places other than the old-fashioned dream of the suburban semi-D.

They may not be able to build a house, but they are rapidly rebuilding the economy in their own image. And that, of course, is drawing the eye of the big-money businesses that are always keen for fresh consumers to exploit.

Part I

Adult Interrupted

Slipping Away

As a rule, I don't walk up to strangers to ask them personal questions – especially when they're wielding a hatchet. I make an exception in this case though and, thankfully, it turns out that the stranger, Ben, is the friendly and approachable type. In fact, he's only too happy to talk to me about the situation he's in.

Ben is 28 years old and he is currently living at home with his parents. He tells me that this living arrangement had been manageable for a long time but, the older he's getting, the more frustrating he's finding it.

'It feels a bit like you're still 16,' he says. 'You're almost having to tip-toe around the place.'

The problem is that he doesn't see any prospect of being able to get out and find a home of his own in the near – or even distant – future. And he's already given it a good shot. Until recently Ben was in a relationship and, as that progressed, the young couple decided to take things to the next level and find a place of their own to rent. But, even with two incomes, that just wasn't possible.

Instead, they found that there wasn't much on the market in or near their price range – and any promising thing that did materialise on listings sites was snapped up almost immediately. Even the pokiest of places in less-than-ideal locations were out of reach for the two. It was a frustrating and fruitless process – one that Ben, ultimately, came away from with even less than when he began. Having started out with thoughts of getting serious – sharing a home, sharing bills, sharing toilet-cleaning duties – the rental recon ended with a break-up. In Ben's view, the stress and disappointment of the process contributed significantly to that.

He's visibly frustrated by the whole thing – and as much dejected as he is angry. Maybe it goes some way to explaining why he's taken up hatchet-throwing as a hobby.

I met Ben at Axe Club Dublin, which is based in an old commercial unit that's tucked away at the end of a red-brick bungalow-lined cul-de-sac, just next to the Royal Canal on the north side of Dublin city centre. As the name suggests, it's a place where people come to throw axes (and sometimes other pointy objects) at wooden targets – which, I can attest, is trickier but also more rewarding than you'd expect. It was established in 2017 by nature guide Heath Dawson – who had already spear-headed an axe-throwing spot in Glendalough in Wicklow – and English engineer Matt Levell who, having discovered the sport shortly after his arrival in Ireland, immediately saw its potential appeal. And as off-the-beaten-track as it may be – both in terms of location and activity – Axe Club has become a popular spot for everything from parties to team-building events to daters – who clearly want to inject a small amount of controlled danger into proceedings.

It's the weekly members' tournament which has brought me here on this Tuesday evening, though – drawing in a decent-sized crowd of axe-chucking devotees. The group skews male – but not nearly as much as you probably think – with the ages ranging from their early 20s through to their mid-to-late 40s. As part of the weekly tournament entrants throw their hatchets three times for six rounds in an attempt to build up as many points as they can. Despite the competitive nature of the night – and the very manly-man impression that axe throwing might conjure up – the diverse crowd gives off a fairly relaxed vibe. Players are quick to cheer for others when they hit the five-point marker – and they laugh off the odd occasion when the vibrations from someone else's axe knocks theirs out of the target. In truth, the closest anyone comes to being combative is when I forget to do the customary 'clinking of axes' before a round of throws.

When all is said and done, the scores are totted up and a winner announced – and that's it. The members then spend a bit of time having a few free throws at the targets, offering them the opportunity to fine-tune their axe-throwing trick shots. At the target next to mine, one of the members tries to get a pick-axe head to stick in the target. And meanwhile, I discover that I fare better when throwing the hatchet 'backwards' (with the blade pointing towards my shoulder when I release it). I also find that throwing the axe as hard as you can is not a great way to score points – in fact, it's more likely to end with your hatchet on the floor.

At the end of the day, though, it's a pretty good way to relieve a bit of stress.

'It's good for getting the frustration out,' Ben jokes. That might explain why he has been coming here more often in recent months – and why he travels across the city every week (battling rush-hour traffic in the process) in order to make the members' meet-up.

Of course, he would still like to get his own place – somewhere he and his friends can congregate, that he can set up in whatever way he wants. But, having already tried and failed to find a rental property – and now facing an even tougher challenge given the fact that he only has one income to work with – he doesn't hold out much hope for that happening anytime soon. And while he is trying to save money, the idea that he would ever be able to afford to buy his own place seems particularly unrealistic in the current market. So, he is facing the prospect of remaining stuck in his parents' house for the foreseeable future. Not being too happy with that, Ben tells me he's considering emigrating to Australia – quite possibly in a matter of months. After all, as far as he's concerned, there's not a whole lot encouraging him to stay in Ireland and no particular prospect of that changing in the near future. All he needs to do now is find a spot in Sydney that will let him throw an axe or two, and he'll be all set.

They don't know they're born

For some, Ben would be a perfect exemplar of the generation that doesn't know how good they have it: the 'Me-me-me-millennial' – the type that feels like they're entitled to everything and unwilling to put in the kind of hard graft that's required to get ahead in life. If he can't get a place at the moment, he just needs to tough it out for a bit longer – and work a bit harder – until it becomes a possibility.

Perhaps in the eyes of their parents, grandparents – and maybe even older siblings – this generation hasn't had to experience real hardship. They were too young to remember the International Monetary Fund rolling into town to usher in an era of austerity. They certainly haven't had to suffer the living nightmare of staring into the whites of Charlie Haughey's eyes as he told them it was time to tighten their belts. Their problem, it seems, is that they only started paying attention to the world around them when the recovery was in full swing. They've seen that things were on the up and can't understand why their own lives don't seem to be heading in the same direction. As a result, they've no experience of sacrificing luxuries in order to make ends meet – and so they're simply not willing or able to do so in order to achieve their goals.

But now that the economy is roaring ahead again, there's plenty of prosperity and opportunity to go around. So rather than crib and moan, these young 'uns might just need to ease up on the lattes and brunches for a while to get what they want.

Now, I know what you're thinking. This is just more of the usual 'kids these days' crap that every generation has to hear from its elders. Or is it? Can we just dismiss what this generation has to say – or is it worth taking this argument seriously for a moment? Maybe there's a solid case to be made that young Irish people today have all the opportunity they need. After all, Ireland is now one of the richest countries in the world. On a per-person basis, our economy goes toe-to-toe with the gold-rich Swiss, it's comfortably ahead of the mighty Americans and it leaves our former colonial masters in the dust.

Now, some might argue that this is purely down to the accounting trickery of multinational companies – 'Leprechaun Economics', as US economist Paul Krugman dubbed it – which sees huge US firms wash their global cash through the Irish tax system. Admittedly, the fact that Ireland's per-capita wealth is second only to out-and-out tax havens like Monaco and Bermuda lends weight to that argument. Of course, the fact that these companies are using Ireland as a route for their revenues certainly doesn't do our economic performance any harm (certainly not in terms of numbers, though what harm it may be doing to our economy's reputation is a discussion for another day). All of that money flushing through Ireland is in fact adding billions of euro in corporation tax revenue to the government's coffers every year.

But – as successive governments and officials at IDA Ireland, the foreign direct investment agency, have long argued – the contributions of Apple, Meta, Microsoft and Google are far more than an accounting measure. They do real work here, they create value and – most importantly – they employ lots of people. So, their balance sheet exercises are only part of the reason why the state is now taking in far more money than it can spend. In fact, unlike previous times in Ireland's past, all parts of the economy – from Silicon Docks in Dublin all the way to Shop Street in Galway – are practically humming with cash.

That's because more people are employed here than ever before – with 2.77 million people working as of mid-2025. The jobs market is so strong that the country has now been in continual, technical full employment for more than three years.

Those multinationals can take a bow for their part in that – but actually, while they each employ plenty of people, they're only really bit players in the country's employment story. Far more important are the near 400,000 small and medium-sized enterprises (SMEs) that are dotted around the place – that's each and every corner shop, café, supermarket, solicitors office, IT firm, builders and vets. On their own they may only employ a handful of people – but together they make up the real engine of the economy, with a combined workforce that's twice the size of the country's large employers.

And when you have a rapidly growing economy, hundreds of thousands of companies looking to expand and very few people out of work, that tends to create the perfect recipe for rising wages. Sure enough, the result is that the average worker here is now earning more than ever before – including the Bailout Babies.

Average earnings came close to €51,000 last year – a near 40 per cent increase over the last ten years. The scale of the increase is even more pronounced in the so-called 'professions', with people in technology, finance and law enjoying increases of closer to 50–60 per cent in the past decade.

That has put considerably more cash in consumers' pockets, allowing them to spend like lords. In 2023 consumers tapped, swiped and clicked their way to more than €152.7 billion in spending on goods and services – up more than 13 per cent in a year and 79 per cent higher than a decade previously.

Some of that was necessary in order to keep up with rising prices but let's not pretend that inflation gobbled up all of that extra cash pumped into the economy by consumers. A lot of it went on funding the finer things in life as well. For example, nearly €22 billion was spent in restaurants and hotels in 2023. A further €5.4 billion was spent on cigarettes, drugs and alcohol.

Crucially, though, and unlike during the Celtic Tiger years, these outgoings weren't all being put onto the credit card. It was real money that people had to spend and not just an IOU to their future selves. Having learned the lessons of the crash – or maybe it's more accurate to say 'still bearing the scars of the crash' – Irish households have actually done a remarkable job of weaning themselves off the debt drug. We're now behaving like very responsible consumers altogether.

During the dizzying heights of late 2009, the combined debt of Irish households had a higher value than the bloated economy itself. We can thank all of the easy-access credit cards, loans over the phone for a trip to Ibiza and 115 per cent mortgages for a home on a flood plain for that. But today this combined debt represents less than a third of the country's GDP. The growing economy has helped flatten the curve, of course, but debt levels are down in real terms too. In fact, we've done such a good job at cutting our personal debt pile that the country's household debt-to-GDP ratio is now well below the European average. It's even considerably better than that of the supposedly frugal Germans.

We've gotten so good with our money that, not only have we been paying down our debts while still splashing out, we've also been leaving some aside for a rainy day. In recent years Irish households have amassed a gargantuan amount in savings, and the pile just keeps growing.

According to the Central Bank, Irish households had a whopping €163 billion sitting in their bank accounts at the start of this year. That total was boosted significantly over the course of the pandemic when many work-from-home types found themselves almost unable to spend the money they were earning. But they kept saving even after lockdowns were lifted – and continue to do so to this day. The knock-on effect of all this earning, spending and saving is a boost to the Exchequer that goes way beyond corporation tax (as important as that is).

Because we're spending so much, the state is taking in record levels of VAT – the tax that's added to the items we buy every day. Last year the government received more than €21.8 billion in VAT – the fourth consecutive year of record VAT take. The figure even surpassed the amount earned from sales during the debt-fuelled largess of the Celtic Tiger years.

And all of the economy's extra employees – and their rising salaries – also means the amount the country's workers are handing up to the Motherland is soaring. In fact, like VAT, the Exchequer's take of income tax has also hit new highs in each of the past four years. Overall, the amount taken in has nearly doubled in the space of six years. It's the flood of money in those three areas that has allowed the government to spend billions more than they had previously planned, while still setting billions more aside for a rainy day.

But Ireland's success isn't just a financial exercise – it's ahead of the curve in many other, more real-world ways as well.

The new Celtic Revival

While Ireland may not be threatening our Scandinavian peers in the 'equality' stakes, we're faring better than most in that regard. The difference between the income of the country's wealthiest and poorest is below the EU average – and well below what's seen in the likes of Britain and Italy. Ireland's inequality ranking also improves considerably after social transfers are taken into account – suggesting that we do a better job than most when it comes to turning taxes from the 'haves' into social welfare supports for the 'have-nots'.

Ireland's education system is also world-renowned, consistently outranking the vast majority of its European and global peers. It's relatively cheap to progress through, too, all the way to third level. And given that the economy is booming and employment is at a record high, everywhere from the Irish SME, to the deep-pocketed multinational, to the public sector is crying out for talent. That means the current generation of students should have their pick of jobs when they graduate – presuming they don't decide to start their own businesses instead (for which there are plenty of grants and supports, too).

Or maybe they'll opt to pursue a more cultural career path, which is also rich with opportunity at the moment. That's because everything in Ireland, from the arts to sport to cuisine, is firing on all cylinders right now.

This new Celtic Revival is seeing Irish actors like Cillian Murphy, Saoirse Ronan, Paul Mescal and Brendan Gleeson pick up plaudits, nominations and awards on a seemingly weekly basis. It's put Irish-made, Irish-written, Irish-set and Irish-language films in the mix for major awards at 7 of the last 10 Oscar ceremonies. As part of that, Irish animation studios like Cartoon Saloon have gone toe-to-toe with the big beasts like Disney, while others – like Brown Bag – have likely produced some or all of your kids'/ grandkids'/nieces'/nephews' favourite cartoons for Netflix, the BBC and Apple.

The world has been reminded once again of Ireland's literary prowess, with Rooney, Keegan and Lynch picking up the baton from Binchy, O'Brien and Wilde. In the music industry, acts like Hozier, Lankum, CMAT and Kneecap are among the many flying the flag for us internationally. Within sports, Ireland is at the top table in everything from rowing, to boxing, to swimming, to running, to rugby. Even the soccer team isn't looking quite as adrift as was once the case.

Meanwhile our food industry's reputation has gone from strength to strength, with the island currently boasting more Michelin stars than ever before. It's a far cry from cabbage, bacon and spuds (not that there's anything wrong with that).

All of which is to say that Ireland is a land of opportunity – the kind of place previous generations would have emigrated in search of. The fact is there are now very few things a person can do elsewhere that can't be done on these shores.

Young people, surely, just need to show a bit of ambition if they want to take advantage of that.

Bright sparks

But while there may be a thread of thinking among older people that these up-and-comers aren't getting ahead because they're lazy and entitled, there's nothing to suggest that young Irish people are short on ambition. In fact, all the evidence points to the fact that, far from being ungrateful and unmotivated, young people have taken advantage of every opportunity this country has to offer them.

Ireland's education system should be applauded for its low barrier of entry – but that only really matters if there are people willing to make use of that. And young people have done so consistently, making Ireland the best educated country in Europe.

As of 2024, more than half of the country's population had a third-level education – putting us head and shoulders above the EU average. Young people here are also far more likely to be well educated than their older countrymen and women too.

Last year 65 per cent of 25–34-year-olds had a third-level education, according to the Central Statistics Office (CSO), compared to just 44 per cent of people aged 55–59.

And it's not like the remaining 35 per cent simply put their feet up. The vast majority have gone to work in the economy – with many of them pursuing educational opportunities beyond the traditional college campus.

Last year alone more than 9,300 people signed up to apprenticeships – an increase of more than 70 per cent compared to 2020. This figure translates into 30,000 people doing in-work training for a range of careers – many of which are consistently in high demand.

And, unsurprisingly, those that take up more training are less likely to be unemployed.

Just 2 per cent of college graduates were unemployed in mid-2024, while the rate was 3 per cent among those with a post-Leaving Certificate qualification. That compares to an unemployment rate of 5 per cent among people with a Leaving Cert only (which, it should be said, is still very low by international standards).

So, while young people have been given every opportunity, they've clearly done what was expected of them and made the most of what's on offer. They've pursued educational opportunities in areas that make them supremely employable. And so, as they've entered the jobs market, it's probably not unreasonable for them to have expected some reward for that. After all, as we already know, the country is currently lousy with deep-pocketed multinationals desperate for skilled workers who are willing to pay handsomely to bring them on board. And that's not to mention those hundreds of thousands of Irish SMEs that are trying to keep up with the big guys.

It sounds like the perfect time for well-educated graduates to arrive on the scene. They should have little trouble in landing the jobs they want – and ones that pay well. Certainly, you'd expect this kind of job to pay as well, if not better, than jobs undertaken by their (less-educated) predecessors a few years ago. And they certainly should be earning the kind of salary that would put them onto the next rung of the adulting ladder that sees them move towards a home, a relationship, a family.

And yet, the statistics are not borne out by reality – that's just not what's happening because all of Ireland's positive indicators hide the reality that the bailout – and the wider financial crisis – broke the country's economic escalator.

Post-Millennial man

Let's for a second imagine every Tinder user's worst nightmare – a distinctly average 20-something male. His bio tells us he played county, he loves dogs and he hates dramas. But (arguably more importantly) the CSO data tells us that he has a third-level educa-tion and a decent job – maybe working admin in an SME.

But the CSO can help us to delve a little bit deeper on what you might call this 'bang-average' specimen. Because it has also published other data that tells us that this 25–29-year-old earned around €43,250 in 2023. That's before any taxes, duties or levies are taken away. Compared to the same 'average' guy in the same age bracket all the way back in 2013, that's a 47 per cent increase in income. Not bad at all. And that also happens to make this age category the one with the biggest percentage increase in earnings over the past decade.

It all sounds very impressive, doesn't it?

Now, Tinderman is still earning well below what his older (less-educated) peers are making – but that's probably to be expected. After all, what they lack in formal education, they make up for in years of experience. Right? The problem is, though, he's not just earning less than his older peers. It turns out that his type is actually losing ground on them.

The average 30–39-year-old earned almost €55,700 in 2023, for example. That gives them a €12,400 advantage on the average earned by their Tinderman colleagues. But back in 2013, the 30-somethings would have been earning more than €40,000 – compared to the €30,500 being brought in by the Tinderman-types of that era (though back then they probably would have been known as OkCupidmen).

That's just north of a €10,000 advantage – meaning the gap was considerably smaller than it is today.

Now it could be argued that, when inflation is taken into account, €10,000 back in 2013 is pretty much the same as €12,000 in 2023. Therefore, they have not really lost ground in terms of their earning power. But even accepting that, it means this cohort – at best – has only held its ground compared to its older colleagues. That's despite the fact that they are better educated than the equivalent worker would have been in the 2010s, and probably better educated than their older colleagues today. And it's despite the economy being in far, far better shape than it was back then, too. It's a similar story when you compare them to the country's 40–49-year-olds.

It's also worth noting that the figure for the average earnings of 25–29-year-olds also glosses over the wider gap being experienced within certain professions – particularly those in the civil and public sectors. So, if Tinderman had opted to be, for example, a teacher, nurse or garda, his starting salary would be sitting below the average even for his own age group and he'd be earning a lot less than his equivalent cohort from the 2000s and 2010s who got in on pre-crash contracts.

All of that is to say that, despite getting a better education and the context of a better economy, this average 20-something is stagnating – or even falling behind their older colleagues – when it comes to their earning power. This group is shaping up to be the first generation that does not have a significant improvement in earnings and living standards when compared to its parents. And while this trend was already in motion, the pandemic has helped to copper-fasten it. Younger people were negatively affected by Covid-related restrictions in a disproportionate way – not just socially but professionally (and, by default, financially) too. The lower-paid jobs that this age group tends to start out in were the ones most likely to be lost during lockdowns. And while youth employment has rebounded dramatically since we emerged from that era, all the signs point to the new jobs being less secure and lower paid. That serves to further handicap young people, forcing them to 'return to go' while everyone else on the board continues to move ahead.

This is a recurring theme for Tinderman's generation – they are losing ground at every turn.

After tax, the Tinderman of 2014 would have been taking home roughly €26,000 a year – or €2,166 a month. If this distinctly average person decided to start renting a distinctly 'average' home he would have been expected to pay roughly €785 per month for the privilege back then, according to the Residential Tenancies Board's (RTB's) *Rent Index* report. In other words, he would have been committing a little over 36 per cent of his monthly income to rent.

But by March of this year, the same average rent would have set the same 'average' guy back €1,612 per month, according to the RTB. The costs have more than doubled in a decade – in case you didn't want to do the sums – in a period of time when this kind of person would have seen their income rise by 47 per cent.

The increase in wages suddenly seems less impressive.

Based on an after-tax salary of roughly €35,585, or €2,965 per month, it means that the modern-day Tinderman is now having to set aside 54 per cent of his pay to keep his landlord happy. So, back in 2014, after taxes and rent, an average 20-something would have had €1,381 a month left to play with. Meanwhile today's Tinderman would have €1,353 left – a decade on, he's actually €28 worse off each month. And that's before accounting for inflation.

And if he has aspirations to break free from the rent trap some day and own his own home, he has even more reason to despair. It's no secret that house prices have sky-rocketed over the past decade too. Between August 2014 and August 2024, national property prices rose by more than 98 per cent. Effectively that means that – all things being equal – the amount a would-be first-time buyer would need to scrape together as a deposit today is double what it was ten years ago. And because average incomes haven't risen by anything close to that, while other major costs (like rent) have, more of the income young people have left after their bills are paid has to be squirrelled away if they're to have any hope of buying in the future.

Now, put yourself back in Tinderman's distinctly average-sized shoes for a minute and imagine you are back in 2013. You've decided to take control of your very-average earnings so you can cut loose from your very-average rent bill. With what you have left after your expenses, you decide to set aside €200 a month to save for a deposit. That's nearly 10 per cent of your take-home pay, so a sizeable undertaking – especially if you're already losing another chunk to rent. But while it may be a stretch, you reckon it's do-able. And while it will take you just over eight years to pull together a deposit on a €200,000 house, you know it will be worth it in the end.

Suddenly, there's a flash of light. You've skipped forward ten years. You're sad to have missed out on a decade of your life but you're delighted to find you've stuck to your savings plan. And so, with €24,000 sitting in your savings account (by rights it should be higher, but savings rates were crap) soon you expect to find yourself on your very average couch in your very average house, binge-watching *The Office* for the 15th time.

Instead, because of the way house prices have gone, you find you're still renting and somehow still €15,600 short of your goal of having a deposit for a distinctly average home.

If only you'd resisted the temptation to buy those 3,280 lattes.

Generation Bart

'I don't want any damn vegetables,' says Todd, as he gives his shocked parents a defiant, squinting side-eye stare. He's picked up his potty mouth from his neighbour but that's no excuse – it's just cost him his beloved bedtime Bible stories.

If this doesn't make any sense to you, perhaps you didn't spend an unnatural amount of your childhood watching *The Simpsons*. This scene is from an episode that first aired in 1992 – but it's been kept alive to this day thanks to endless repeats, YouTube clips, streams and memes. It's become so iconic that it's the moment Cliona – who was born around the same time that this *Simpsons* scene first aired – has chosen to immortalise on a hand-painted bowl.

I get talking to her at the Dublin Pottery Painting Studio near Smithfield in the capital's city centre, where people can come to paint everything from mugs to bowls to egg-cups to picture frames. The evening sessions are a bring-your-own-beer affair and, while people are free to paint whatever they want, there's usually a theme of some kind to offer attendees artistic inspiration. Tonight is *Simpsons* night – and to get everyone in the mood there's a projector showing clips from its hundreds of episodes, as songs from the show's 36-year run play on the shop's speakers. In a few minutes, there'll be a *Simpsons*-themed quiz and Sinéad, who's managing the event, tells me that – following complaints about how easy the questions were at the last *Simpsons*-themed event – she's worked particularly hard to make them trickier this time around.

She's not wrong, either. Before coming here I'd have fancied my chances in a *Simpsons* quiz – but I immediately find myself floundering when asked what pseudonym Bart uses to respond to Mrs Krabappel's singles ad (when I check afterwards, I realise this is actually from the same episode as Todd's vegetable rebellion – and the answer is 'Woodrow Wilson'). But plucking out this bit of knowledge is no bother to Cliona or her boyfriend Joe. This is their second time at the *Simpsons*-themed pottery painting night. They were also at a separate *Simpsons* quiz just a few weeks ago – so, it's fair to say that while they're technically younger than Maggie, they're fans of the show nonetheless.

'It's just something different rather than going out and doing the same stuff – it just puts a bit of a twist on it,' says Joe.

It's also a chance for them to get out of their respective houses. Both are still living at home with their parents – and both Cliona and Joe have a sibling who's still in the same house with them too. They're living like this despite the fact that Joe is a full-time, fully qualified plumber who's out the door with work at the moment. Cliona is in her final months of college and working part time but they're still not earning enough to make moving out an option.

'We looked at renting and it's just not feasible,' says Joe. 'I'm full time, earning good money but it's not enough … so it's a choice between renting and doing nothing, or else live at home and be able to go out.'

No place like home
The constant shifting of the goalposts – or, maybe more accurately, shrinking of the goal itself – has pushed homeownership further and further out of reach for people like Joe and Cliona. It's not necessarily impossible but for most it's fairly close to that. Going back to Tinderman and his heroic effort to save €200 a month for 10 years, for example, he could still put that decade of savings towards a deposit on a €200,000 house, just like he had planned.

The catch is that he'd probably have to move to Leitrim in order to make that happen. And, while it's not my place to speculate on the reasons why, the statistics suggest that many people are simply not willing to do that. In fact, one recent statistic from an Airbnb study suggested that more Irish people had made the effort of travelling to Asia than had gone up (or down) the road to Leitrim.

As a result, we now have a growing, and ageing, demographic that are yet to set foot on the property ladder. According to the Census, there were 36,549 people aged 25 to 29 who owned their own home back in 2011. That meant that just over 10 per cent of people in that age bracket in that year were homeowners. (More than 3,200 of them had no mortgage, either. And I'm sure everyone was delighted for them and wasn't even the slightest bit envious – not one bit).

But by 2022, the number of homeowning 25–29-year-olds had more than halved to 15,849. That's 5.4 per cent of that age group. In other words, the 20-something homeowner has rapidly become an anomaly. The likes of Cliona and Joe – both still locked out of homeownership – are now very much the norm.

The same shrinking trend is reflected as you move up the ages, too. Among 30–34-year-olds, more than 95,400 people owned a home in 2011 – which is close to a quarter of that age group. Just five years later the numbers had fallen below 59,000 (or 16.3 per cent of this bracket). By 2022, the number had dipped to less than 50,000 (or less than 15 per cent of people in this age category). Even the part of the population that's approaching middle age has, to a lesser extent, been vulnerable to this shift. In 2011, almost 121,350 (or a third of) 35–39-year-olds had their own home. By 2016 it was 106,500 (or just over 27 per cent). By 2022 it was 92,000 (or 24 per cent).

Having once been par for the course, nowadays anyone under 40 who has managed to buy their own place surely feels like they nabbed a seat on the last chopper out of Vietnam. But even among those who managed to get a foot on the property ladder, an increasing proportion of them were only able to do so because they were given a leg-up by someone else.

A 2024 survey by the National Youth Council of Ireland (NYCI) found that, of the 18–29-year-olds who had already purchased their own home, more than half had received financial support from the Bank of Mam and Dad in the process. Meanwhile, a broader survey of first-time buyers by Banking and Payments Federation Ireland found that more than 1 in 10 were relying on inheritance gifts to pad out their deposit.

That doesn't just highlight how much harder it's become for someone trying to get a foothold on the property market, it also represents a further skewing of the market away from the less well-off. Working your way out of disadvantage, getting into a well-paying job and saving your arse off is no longer enough to guarantee your own home – because if you don't also have a decent amount of generational wealth backing you up, there's a far greater chance you'll find yourself being outbid time and time again. This growing challenge has rapidly accelerated what was a previously gradual trend, which has seen young home-owners go from the norm to a rarity.

Back in 1991, the age at which more people than not had become homeowners was 26. By 2006, this had slipped to 28. That's not a dramatic shift over a 15-year period, it has to be said, but the pace of change has accelerated from that point on. By 2011, the Census tells us it was taking most people until 32 to own their own home. By the last Census in 2022, the cross-over point had shifted again – to 36.

There's an added significance to this slide in the age of first-time buyers. Banks here tend only to offer mortgage terms that bring customers up to their mid-to-late 60s – essentially to avoid the risk of pensioners being asked to cover hefty monthly repayments. That means that, once they hit their mid-30s, most would-be buyers are up against the clock in terms of the maximum duration of the mortgage they can get. Every extra year that they need to spend saving and building up their income represents one year less that they can borrow for. The amount they can borrow from the bank may not, in theory, change, but it gets squashed into a shorter and shorter window. That means the repayment costs rise – potentially hitting against the upper limit of what they can afford to dole out each month.

Euro vision

It is worth pointing out that Irish people are not the only ones watching the prospect of property ownership slip away from them. The trend is being replicated in many other countries and cities around the world, from Asia, to Europe, to the United States. After all, both the financial crisis and the pandemic were global phenomena and both had a globally distorting effect on property markets and young people's earnings prospects.

But just as Ireland was one of the hardest hit in the world by the financial crash, so too has it been hardest hit by the hangover that's come behind it. For example, between 2010 and 2023, property prices in the countries using the euro rose by 41 per cent – a not insignificant change. In the same period in Ireland, prices rose by 59 per cent. The comparison is even less favourable when you look at the pace of growth in Ireland compared to the major economies like France (+31 per cent) or Spain (+9.8 per cent) or Italy (prices actually fell 8.2 per cent in the period there).

But it is also worth pointing out that the shift in home-ownership among young adults is in the context of a culture that has, traditionally, been unusually keen on buying its own place (thanks, colonialism!). From one perspective, having the average buyer get onto the property ladder in their mid-30s rather than mid-20s only brings us in line with our European neighbours – where renting tends to be seen more as a destination in itself rather than a stop-gap on the way towards a mortgage. And while the slippage in the average age of a first-time buyer has probably come at a faster pace than many expected, it is, of course, the case that many would-have-been-buyers have instead ended up embracing their European side by heading into the rental market.

The Irish rental market is not comparable to continental Europe's, though. In many countries renters have far more security, access to longer leases and the option to make a place their own. And it's not as though the Irish rental market represents an easier – or even cheaper – option for people who can't yet buy a home of their own. The dramatic rise in rental prices means that route is quickly becoming closed to many younger people too and becoming a trap to others. Again, while rising rents has also been a feature in other European countries, Ireland has fared far worse than the average. Average rent prices across the euro area rose by a little over 20 per cent between 2010 and 2023 – while Ireland saw its rents rise by more than 100 per cent in the same period.

And so, when more young people have found themselves blocked from getting on the property ladder, the proportion of 25–39-year-olds who are renting has also fallen. Depending on which section of that age range you look at, you can see a different story at play.

The 25–29-year-olds

You might consider this age range to be a prime renter demographic – right? In fact, there is a pronounced shift away from renting among those aged between 25 and 29. Nearly a quarter of this age group were in the rental market in 2011. That's close to 86,000 people, to put a real number on it. But by 2022, the number and percentage had fallen sharply with less than 18.5 per cent or 54,600 people in this age category counting themselves as renters.

The 30–34-year-olds

The number of renters here fell by more than 10,000 over the same 11-year period, though that can be partially explained by the fact that the overall number of people in this age bracket also fell in the period, due to the country's ageing population. In fact, the proportion of renters in this age group actually rose slightly. But remember that this was at the same time that this age group was seeing a dramatic fall in homeownership. That is not remotely made up for in the modest rise in the proportion of renters, meaning only a tiny number of the tens of thousands who were not getting on the property ladder were taking up rental options as an alternative. And it meant that while 45 per cent of 30–34-year-olds were homeowners or renters in 2011, just over 36 per cent could say the same by 2022.

The 35–39-year-olds

In the past, renters in this age group were a relatively rarity. In 2011, there were 59,470 people aged 35 to 39 who declared themselves to be renters – just over 16 per cent of the group's total population. In fact, the Census data from that year shows, as might be expected, that people increasingly slipped from the rental market to a mortgage as they moved through their 20s and 30s. But that trend had slowed considerably by 2022 when almost 74,600 people aged 35 to 39 were still renting. That represents 19.5 per cent of that cohort. And this indicates that the late-30s types who would have bought a home by now are being kept out of the market for longer than before. The main thing that differentiates them from their 20-something colleagues is that they have better earnings and so more of them can continue to afford to rent.

But, of course, that's not universally true because the increase in rental numbers within that age group doesn't totally account for the fall in homeownership over the same period – either in terms of the percentage or real terms. That means there are still thousands who are not buying but are also not renting either.

Combining the rental figure with the falling number of home-owners, it means less than a quarter of this age group were paying a mortgage or rent by 2022. That compares to more than a third back in 2011.

And when you put all of those figures together, it means that while you had nearly 43 per cent of 25–39-year-olds in a place of their own (rented or bought) back in 2011, there were just over 35 per cent in the same position by 2022.

So, if you have fewer young adults owning their own homes, or even taking the decision to rent, where are they living?

In some cases, the answer is 'in another country' (more on that later). But with many others, it's Casa Del Mam and Dad.

Home sweet (?) home

Cliona and Joe are a prime example of this phenomenon – with both still living at home with their respective parents. And while Joe tells me that they each get on well with their other half's folks, it's still – understandably – a less-than-ideal situation. Living at home as an adult means you're almost sitting on top of the rest of the family, he says, or confined to your room for the night. Not exactly a dream scenario for someone trying to start their adult lives – not to mention a blossoming romance.

And while it's going to be cold comfort to them, at least they can console themselves with the fact that they're not alone. Others I speak to are also still at home despite being in good jobs and good relationships. Some couples are living together – sometimes in a granny flat in one set of parents' garden, but often they're just in one of the spare bedrooms. Needless to say, no-one I speak to is particularly happy with the situation – except, perhaps, the builder who tells me he's out the door adding extensions, convert-ing garages and attics and building garden rooms to cater for all of these unexpected guests. And I suspect he's going to have plenty of work in that area for the foreseeable future.

According to the most recent Census, there were more than 522,000 adults living with their parents. That is a 19-per-cent increase on the same figure for 2011, meaning that, in the space of 11 years, the number of adult children living with their parents increased by 83,000. ('Adult children living with their parents' is a bit of a mouthful so, from now on, let's call them Box Room Occupiers – or BROs for short.)

Now some of these BROs will have just turned 18 – and in fairness, it would have been unusual, even in the 1990s, for people to have flown the nest at that age. Instead, it's long been the trend that young people here would start migrating from their parents' abode in their early 20s and most of them would have been gone, one way or another, by their mid-20s. That does still happen but the changes now occur at a glacial pace, with a much longer tail on the end.

Back in 2011, almost 54 per cent of 20–24-year-olds were still living with their parents. By 2022, more than 61 per cent of that cohort were still at home. In real terms, that means there were over 187,000 people in this age group who were still at home in 2022 – around 25,000 more than was the case in 2011. By the time people had hit the 25–29-year-old category, the percentage who were still at home in 2022 had fallen to a third. Which, on the face of it, is a significant move in the right direction. In comparison, though, back in 2011, just a quarter of them would still have been sitting in the parental homestead. In real terms, that's about 10,000 more late-20s BROs in the space of 11 years.

It's worth bearing in mind that the Census figures for numbers of adult children living at home do not include students living away from home during their studies, nor do they include young adults living with their partners' parents while trying to save for a deposit or the many who have left the country faced with no alternative but the box room. That all means that Irish people are now leaving the home – either to emigrate, buy or rent – at an older age than would have been the case before. And, just like with house prices and rental costs, we're faring worse than our European neighbours.

Back in 2010, the average Irish person moved out of their parents' place at 25 – ahead of the EU average of around 27. Just a decade later, the script had flipped and Irish people weren't getting out of the homestead until they were gone 28 – compared to the EU average of 26. In 2014, less than a quarter of our 18–24-year-olds were still living at home. That compared to the EU average of 33.4 per cent and made Ireland one of the region's best in terms of getting the grown-up kids out the door. By 2023, more than 42 per cent of the same age group still lived at home in Ireland – compared to the EU average of 37 per cent. Suddenly even the Italians are joking about us being a bunch of mamma's boys.

And while it's easy to lose sight of the fact in the face of all of these averages and generalities, each one of those extra nest-dwellers actually represents multiple frustrated lives. It's not just the people who are stuck in their parents' houses that suffer but also the parents who are having to put them up indefinitely.

'It's probably not the trajectory that they envisioned – maybe they would like to have their own space as well,' says Niamh Delmar, who is a chartered counselling psychologist in Co. Wicklow.

While I think it's fair to say that, for the most part, the parents are not as frustrated as their adult children. One side has to put their plans for their entire future on hold. The other is only having to postpone their plans for a home gym. One group is being blocked from leaving their adolescence for the foreseeable future. The other is being blocked from walking around the house in the nip for a few more years.

Still, it is the case that both sides are having to delay their plans. Having your life on hold like that can have a somewhat hard-to-quantify impact on a young adult and can warp the dynamic between the generations.

Regression therapy

Have you ever run into an old school teacher? If you have, you might have noticed a funny – but far from unusual – thing happening. Suddenly you find your posture improving somewhat, you become more aware of how you're speaking. Reflexively, you find yourself saying 'sir' or 'miss'. This could be a teacher you had a good relationship with at the time and it might be years since you were their student. Maybe you've gone to college and gotten an education beyond anything they could have taught you. Maybe you've gotten a well-paying job where you have responsibility for very important, very expensive things. Perhaps you even have kids of your own, who are half-way through the education system themselves. But none of that really matters because the minute you see that teacher, or hear their voice, you're back in the classroom. You're only short of nervously adjusting the tie you haven't worn in years.

This is what's known in psychology as 'regression' – a phenomenon that sees us mentally and emotionally revert to an earlier stage in our lives. It can happen in response to a traumatic event or shock or it can be triggered by something as small as an environmental change, like a return to old surroundings. This happens in families – and it doesn't take much time kick in. It's the reason why beyond-middle-aged siblings, who are otherwise sensible and serious people, can break into childish squabbling within minutes of sharing a room again. And it's the reason why they can suddenly be silenced when scolded by their mother or father (much to the amusement of the onlooking grandchildren). It can be a jarring experience for people – and the tension it creates helps to explain why family get-togethers can sometimes be more stressful than they should.

While dealing with this over the course of a meal – or even a weekend-long visit – can be tricky, doing it constantly is a real challenge. It's even harder when there is no clear dividing line which signals when the relationship between a parent and child needs to become a relationship between adults – never mind there being any clear guide on what exactly that change means. The reality is that parents never stop parenting and many struggle to adjust their concept of 'parenting' as the years go by.

'There are parents who, in many ways, over-cosset their kids,' says Stephanie Regan, a clinical psychologist who specialises in relationships, health and wellbeing. 'They can do that at 12, they even can do it at 20, they can do it at 30.

'Some of what you do for your child is helpful and then there comes a point where you get negative returns. If you are doing so much for them that you are weakening their confidence in their own ability to do something, then you're in a toxic, negative kind of arrangement.'

As Stephanie says, there is no hard rule about when a parent–child relationship needs to change; it can be a gradual thing, and it can differ from person to person. Some will be ready for independence at 18; for others it might take until they're 28.

'But there comes a point where you are really wanting to do it on your own – it's a natural impetus, almost like the sexual impetus where you get to a point where you're interested in other people,' she says.

Part of that involves people turning to their peers – rather than their parents – for advice and moral guidance. It likely also sees them comparing themselves more to friends rather than family. But that change can easily be missed by parents and often it requires the child deciding to leave home to jolt them out of the over-parented trap. That change ideally creates a line in the sand –

and a new dynamic – that the parent–child relationship can move towards. The old parent–child relationship may still exist in the context of the family home, but the new living arrangement may allow parents to see their child as their own person – one who is (hopefully) showing that they are able to look after themselves. Likewise, flying the coop can help the child to take a step closer to self-sufficiency and, in time, perhaps view their parents as something other than the rule-setters.

'When people talk about independence, I suppose it's independence of thought, of social life,' says Stephanie. 'But I think it's more internally too, like making good, independent decisions, taking responsibility for all of that.

'But also, for me, it's about confidence – because at some deep level, there's a sense that "I'm not where I should be".'

Unfortunately, though, the housing crisis is interrupting the normal rules of growing up. If the child is not able to make that move – even when they're ready and willing – and they are forced to stay in the same room they played in when they were 10, it can be tricky to create a new dynamic. It's hard to break the habits that have built up over 18+ years of practice, leaving the existing relationship as the dominant one and the child in a regressed state.

Regression can manifest in any number of ways. It may be as simple as the parent resuming (or continuing to do) household chores on behalf of their adult child – like fixing their dinner and washing their clothes. Possibly in cases where their child had been easily managing that by themselves beforehand. Now, having your dinner handed to you and your washing done every day might not sound like the worst fate in the world. Perhaps it may go towards explaining why, in a 2021 CSO survey, 57 per cent of adults living with their parents said they enjoyed the circumstances they were in and 62 per cent of them even said they would miss their parents if they lived apart.

The parents were upbeat about the whole experience too, it should be said. According to the CSO, 87 per cent of them said they enjoyed living with their adult child (or children), while 73 per cent said they would miss them if they lived elsewhere.

But while being waited on and minded may be a silver lining in this kind of arrangement, it can come at a heavy psychological cost. Having your dinner made for you also means you may have less agency in terms of what you eat and when you eat it. A small thing, perhaps, but it's a symptom of a bigger malaise. More importantly, though, young people can miss out on what Stephanie calls 'micro-challenges' – the countless small decisions that are a cornerstone of being a grown up.

'Paying your own bills, finding people to live with and having those nights that are sort of aimless and unmonitored,' she says. 'That's a challenge. That's a social challenge – all these things allow you to grow.

'And they might sit in an apartment they're sharing with someone, and those people cross-check them for not cleaning up after themselves – and it's a kind of reality check; they suck it up and move on, and they learn that that's not okay. That's a very important thing that's missing when you don't move out.'

There's every chance mam and dad get on their case about the same issues at home, but that's not nearly the same as hearing it from a peer. Your parents are just being annoying; your house-mate might have a point. Missing out on little things like that – the challenges and opportunities of living alone – means that the adult child can find themselves occupying a passive and subservient role at home. That might be the case even where they take on significant responsibilities and agency in their work lives and personal relationships. Meanwhile parents – even those who realise their child no longer technically needs their input – might still struggle not to interfere, critique or generally butt into their offspring's life.

Being bound to the family food schedule can also add to the constant rows about cleaning up after yourself and household chores and yells up the stairs to lower that music down and 'What time did you get in at last night?'-type conversations. And that's going to be the case in what would otherwise be considered a healthy family dynamic – and that's not always what young people are facing when they live in the parental home.

'There isn't a fairy-tale family out there,' says Niamh. 'There can be other implications for a person being stuck at home, especially if there's a difficult parent, or there's an issue with alcoholism.'

Or, she says, it may be that the dynamic between the parents has deteriorated and the adult child is stuck in the middle of that growing domestic tension. Often these are the kinds of factors that would prompt a young adult to cast off on their own as quickly as possible, but if the financial realities of getting their own place don't make that possible, they end up being stuck in an increasingly toxic arrangement. And while the home may, in the past, have been little more than a staging post in their day-to-day activities, this is all happening at a time when it has a more central role in many other aspects of a young person's life.

'If they're going into work every day there's a break away from the family,' says Niamh. 'But now you might have parents who are just recently retired or are working from home, and then they have their son or daughter working from home, taking up a room – maybe not the bedroom – and all of that carries additional pressures as well.' This can all chip away at their confidence and undermine the adult they're trying to become. Inevitably, it also becomes a major source of frustration for everyone involved.

'[People in this situation feel] helpless, stress, the stress of trying,' says Stephanie. 'When stress becomes relentless it can often become depressing. We can all stress up for a while and get something done – you know, suck it up, be with your parents for two years, save your money, get it done. But if you can't do that, that becomes a relentless kind of stress … and it morphs into a form of depression.'

So, young adults who want to and are trying to stake a claim as their own person, increasingly don't see an end in sight. They are facing down the prospect of being treated like a child – with their comings and goings monitored informally ('What time do you call this?') or even policed ('Don't be getting home at all hours tonight') – for the foreseeable future. Even with the best of intentions, it can be difficult to have any real privacy in this kind of house-share situation too (and the best of intentions are not always at play).

It should be said too that parents who might have been looking forward to the finish line of their child's adulthood and dared to dream of the freedoms an empty nest might bring have reason to despair too – especially if their adult child has regressed to the time when they weren't able to load the dishwasher or washing machine. And it's likely for this reason that, while the majority of both adult children and parents told the CSO that they were enjoying living together and would miss each other when the arrangement came to an end, most are still looking forward to a time when they are not living in the same space.

According to its 2021 survey, half of the parents who were asked said they would prefer it if their children lived somewhere else. It was a far more resounding vote for separation from the adult children, though, with almost 9 out of 10 wishing they were somewhere else. Going some way towards explaining that is the fact that more than half of the children surveyed said their parents would not treat them like an adult until they moved out.

Even among those stuck in this perpetual parent–child dynamic there is another sub-group that is perhaps the worst affected of all: families that went through the 'normal' process of the adult child moving on to their own place, only for them to move back in years later. The 2024 NYCI *State of our Young Nation* survey found that 11 per cent of the 18–29-year-olds who were living with their parents had returned within the past two years. That rose to nearly a quarter of people among those aged 27 to 29 (though the survey notes that this is based on a relatively small pool of respondents in that age group). In these cases, the young adults would have managed to go it alone and had the opportunity and time to build their independence and their own lives. At the same time their parents would have gotten used to having a bit more space (and maybe money) than they did before … only for that new reality to be wiped out.

People talk a lot about the Boomers but we should all spare a thought for the Boomerangers.

Cartoon kids

Of course, you could argue that there is a third way. Just because an adult child is living at home, it doesn't mean that they have to be treated like an infant. And that is true. Stephanie points out that a child transitioning to adulthood isn't necessarily dependent on them moving out – even if it can be helpful to some.

But even for those who may want to embrace a fresh dynamic, finding a readjustment that suits everyone is not easy. After all, there is an automatic imbalance between the owner of the house and the person who is, for all intents and purposes, a tenant. And the parent is entitled to set boundaries, rules and expectations within their home. Perhaps the challenge comes in accepting that the adult child is entitled to set boundaries of their own. Depending on their parenting style over the years, this could be an alien concept to some.

'There are healthy ways to live together with parents,' she says. 'You need to have a new kind of deal with your kids – because they're not kids anymore. You're sharing a house now, perhaps with another couple.'

The advice is that families need to sit down and have an open conversation about what they want and what they expect, which probably doesn't come naturally to Irish people. But, assuming you can get over the discomfort of being upfront and honest, it's then a question of agreeing a middle ground between those two points that keeps everyone happy – or happy enough.

'You've got your old roles – but it's a new time and a new division,' Stephanie says.

Achieving this is no mean feat, of course. Even where the parents' rules might be fairly reasonable, they're likely still going to be more restrictive than the rules a young adult would adhere to in their own place. That may come down to something as simple as being able to leave the dirty dishes until tomorrow morning, without fear of it becoming a major flash point. And really, no matter what the rules or expectations are at home, the young adult is going to find living with their parents a frustrating experience – purely by definition. The fact that they're there automatically means that they're not making the kind of progress in their life goals that they would like. Or, at the very least, that the path towards their goals is a lot harder – or slower – than they would like it to be. That could be made even worse if they see any of their peers managing to get a place of their own.

Regardless of how they are being treated at home, though, things are not going the way they want. And the longer they're stuck at home, the more frustrating that gets. What that's leading to is a growing generation of lost boys and girls – who are no longer children but not quite yet adults either. They might have a proper job but, through no fault of their own, they haven't had to budget to ensure they are fed and watered from one end of the month to the other. They might fancy themselves as mature, but they've never had that truly tested – for example, through experiencing the crushing tragedy of having to hand over hundreds of euro of hard-earned cash for a new washing machine.

In his 1983 book, American psychoanalyst Dr Dan Kiely wrote about the rising number of young men he was seeing in his practice who seemed unwilling to grow up and accept the responsibilities of adulthood. These selfish and narcissistic teens went on to become selfish and narcissistic adults, he said, who struggled in their professional and personal relationships. He coined the term 'Peter Pan syndrome' to describe the phenomenon.

In more recent years, his concept has been used by some to refer to the growing demographic of young adults who have not yet started to develop lives that are truly independent of their parents: the Peter Pan generation. It's probably not the best analogy, though. J.M. Barrie's Peter Pan was the boy who *wouldn't* grow up – not the boy who couldn't. A more fitting comparison for this generation would be a character who – through no fault of their own – does not grow up, no matter how much time passes and no matter what they do in their lives. Which brings us right back to where we started: arguably this generation has more in common with Bart and Lisa Simpson than Peter Pan.

No Sex Please, We're Young(ish)

According to the *Oxford English Dictionary*, the opposite of an 'aphrodisiac' is an 'anaphrodisiac'. The *Urban Dictionary* offers the somewhat punchier 'boner killer'.

But whatever words you use, it doesn't take a relationship expert to see why spending more of your early adult life in your parents' box room is going to be a bit of a downer when it comes to dating. 'Your place or mine?' rolls off the tongue in a way that 'Your mam and dad's place or my mam and dad's place?' simply does not. Ending your first date with 'Would you like to come in for coffee?' probably has a slightly higher chance of success than asking them 'Would you like to come in to meet my dad?' And, of course, that's assuming that bringing a first date back to the family home is a viable option at all.

That's a kind-of deal-breaker for Ellie, who's 29 years old. I say kind-of, because it's a stance that she's clearly grappling with the rights and wrongs of. 'I'm out renting … and I would love someone who's at the same stage as me – you know, I don't want to meet your parents immediately,' she said. 'But is that fair of me to expect that in a housing crisis that's out of people's control?'

I meet Ellie – an occupational therapist and part-time stand-up comedian – at a Pitch a Friend dating event. As the name suggests, the format of the night sees people pitch their friends as potential partners to attendees via the extremely romantic medium of the PowerPoint presentation. It's organised by Gráinne O'Hogan who, having found herself single last year, quickly realised the horrors of the dating app experience. Looking for an alternative, she stumbled across the Pitch a Friend event, which had become a fixture of the Chicago dating scene. She contacted its creator, Lucas Chaufournier, to see if it would be possible for her to adopt the concept in Ireland, and he gave her his blessing (actually, he did more than that – going so far as to travel to Ireland, with his family, to help Gráinne organise the first event).

Tonight is the second outing for Pitch a Friend's Irish chapter, and Ellie is one of 12 pitchees (she's also a pitcher – returning the favour for her own hype-woman, Erin). And while she is obviously here in the hope that she will find some kind of a romantic connection, at the very least, she's walking away with a bit of reassurance.

'In the last week for me I've had, within my friend group, three pregnancy announcements and two engagements,' she says. 'The most important decision I'm making this week is should I get highlights? There's so much pressure … but seeing this takes some of that pressure off and makes you realise that not everyone is getting engaged and having children.'

And while it is a dating night on the face of it, the Pitch a Friend event definitely feels like it is part group-therapy session too. The room is naturally full of – for the most part – singles who are looking for love, but everyone just seems happy to have found some kindred spirits, if nothing else. I came along wondering if Irish people's unique biology made it possible for them to talk positively and sincerely about their friends – or whether the pitches would descend into a merciless barrage of devastating but ultimately well-meaning insults. What transpires is a series of upbeat, funny and heart-felt advocations for friends and that positivity is reciprocated by the crowd, which is constantly vocal in its support for both the pitchers and the pitchees. In the end, even if they didn't come home with any new phone numbers, no-one was left in any doubt about their dateability.

While that might not seem like an awful lot, as Ellie's example proves, it's something that people need at this time in their lives. Because while it's often under-recognised or even dismissed as a hangover of the uncertainty of their teenage years, young adult-hood is a time of heightened anxiety and uncertainty for most.

Back in 2001, Abby Wilner and Alexandra Robbins wrote about this phenomenon, talking about the 'quarterlife crisis' that they said was facing young adults. Based loosely on Erik Erikson's eight stages of development and echoing the more familiar concept of a midlife crisis, it highlighted the challenge facing 20-somethings who are under pressure on all fronts. They're at a point in their lives when they need to make the right career choices, form the right relationships and keep up with their peers – all while making the most of the freedoms of youth. Bear in mind, this concept was created before Facebook, Instagram, TikTok and Tinder came along to turn the pressure dial up to 11. None of this is necessarily related to the added complication of being stuck in your parents' house well into your 20s and 30s.

Regardless of whether they are still at home, or in their own place, younger adults seem to be finding it harder to form long-term relationships. And while Ellie's friend group might have led her to think she was an outlier, there is no doubt that the Bailout Babies are now taking longer and longer to find 'the one'.

The Census backs this up. From it, we can see that the pro-portion of young people classed as 'single' has grown steadily over the past decade or more. It should be noted that the CSO's definition of 'single' is actually 'someone who hasn't been married', so it doesn't give a full representation of what's hap-pening on the ground, and it's fair to note that there has been a gradual shift in Irish people's attitudes towards marriage – of course people married young when they lived in a society that told them it was the only way they could get the ride *and* go to heaven. Once that particular monkey was off our collective back, the urge to run down the aisle seemed to wane somewhat. That has also led to a slip in the age at which taking the plunge is seen as desirable.

Even bearing all of that in mind – and trying to account for it – we can see that young adults are taking longer and longer to tie the knot. There has been a significant growth in 'singles' – even when comparing the years since we were unburdened from our religious duty to wed.

As recently as post-enlightenment 2011, 96.5 per cent of people aged 20 to 24 were 'single'. So, the vast, vast majority of those in their early 20s were not married. No shock. But by 2022, that had grown to 98 per cent – meaning a wedding at such a young age was fleetingly rare.

In the 25–29 age bracket, just over 80 per cent were unmarried in 2011, showing that things were starting to move on the nuptials front but were still relatively uncommon. By the time we get to 2022, though, 88 per cent of this category were classed as 'single' – a sizeable shift in the trend.

Really though, nowadays, it's the 30s that represent Irish people's wedding era. Not just because you're guaranteed to spend a year or two of this decade travelling to every hotel, country club, guesthouse and boutique barn in the country for various friends' and family members' big days but also because this is the decade in which most say 'I do' (for the first time, anyway).

Back in 2011, just over 53 per cent of people aged 30 to 34 were classed as 'single' by the CSO. That means we're getting achingly close to half of this population group being married off. In the same year, the 35–39-year-old singles of the country would have been considering applying for endangered breed status, as they made up just 34 per cent of this age cohort.

Fast forward to 2022 and the 30–34-year-old singles were still a comfortable majority at over 64 per cent. Amongst those aged 35 to 39, meanwhile, 42 per cent were still classed as single. Put the two groups together and you see that, by 2022, the majority of people in their 30s are unmarried – as opposed to them being a minority group as recently as 2016.

All of this is reflected in the average age of brides and grooms in Ireland. Back in 2003, the average age for Tinderman to graduate from app to aisle was 32.7. His distinctly average bride would have been a bit younger, too, at 30.6. But by 2023, both Tinderman and his Tinderbride were five years older by the time they said 'I do': aged 37.7 and 35.8 respectively. (The silver lining in all of this is that people in their 30s will save a fortune on all the weddings they won't have to go to.)

Out of date

It is fair to say, though, that this does not necessarily mean the country's dating scene has dried up. People may just be opting to keep the knot – in their otherwise committed relationships – untied. But while Ireland's broader shift away from marriage has stemmed from our move away from organised religion, the more recent decline and delay has had less to do with individual choice and more to do with personal circumstances.

Clinical psychologist Stephanie Regan spoke already about how being stuck in their parents' home can knock a young adult's confidence and stunt their social growth, but she goes further to say that the problem can affect their ability to find a mate as well.

'Because it takes confidence to be in a relationship, doesn't it,' she says, 'to, in some way, present yourself or offer yourself as someone who's attractive, interesting, lots to talk about? And so, I think because their confidence gets eroded it shows up there. I think it shows up in that feeling of being out of step with the group, of being behind. It's not a nice feeling.'

Author, columnist and commentator Dr Caroline West, who has a PhD in sexual studies and lectures at University College Cork, says her students often have to leave early because their inability to find student accommodation means they face long commutes to and from their parents' home. 'They have to get the bus and they're spending hours at that, so they don't even have the energy to date – even if they wanted to,' she says.

Research conducted in 2023 by the dating app Bumble found that 30 per cent of its respondents were living at home with their parents at that time. That's actually a considerably higher percentage than is suggested by the Census data I referred to in the last chapter. That data indicated that around 11 per cent of people aged 30 to 39 were living at home with their parents in 2022. This may suggest that the Bumble survey was skewed towards younger respondents who were more likely still to be at home. But more likely it indicates that there is a significant overlap between people who are single (which this survey focused on) and those who are stuck at home. This would make sense, too, given how much harder it is to buy or rent on a single income.

The Bumble survey went further, too. It indicated that 70 per cent of people found it more difficult to date while living at home with their parents (or, indeed, their roommates – after all, there is a significant number of young renters who are actually in house-share situations and dealing with similar challenges to those still stuck at home). Curiously, men found the 'dating while sharing a house with others' situation more difficult than women – 75 per cent compared to 65 per cent.

As for the reasons why so many BROs find dating harder – well, some of them are probably pretty obvious. Not having somewhere private to go back to after a successful date is going to act as a major roadblock to a would-be couple. Having to tip-toe up the stairs and talk in hushed tones, for fear of waking someone – or having to deal with a premature parental introduction – is not exactly an ideal mood-setter.

'It's kind of a case of "Where do you go?"' says Dr West. 'You can't really bring a one-night stand back on your two-hour bus journey to your parents' house – so that makes things a little awkward. You've got people who are a little bit stunted by the lack of experiences that we might have taken for granted as rites of passage. That freedom to be a 21-year-old and make the mistakes you need to, have your heart broken and have those experiences of relationships that really build up that additional maturity.'

The lack of space also hinders the normal lifecycle of a relationship in other ways. Just as Stephanie Regan says, you get to a point where you seek advice and moral guidance from your peers not your parents, the same is probably true when it comes to whatever relationship woes might come your way.

'Even things like going through a break-up – to process that you might want to have time alone to grieve. You don't necessarily want your parents knowing your heart is broken,' says Dr West. 'Your heart might even be broken over a situationship or a one-night stand and you don't want to be telling your parents that.'

This, she says, can have a knock-on effect on how people manage in future relationships too, because by not learning how to process these challenges now, they'll find them harder to deal with in the future.

'They're not learning the art of the apology, how to compromise in a relationship, how to make relationships sustainable, how to reflect on previous relationships,' she says. 'And if they're not getting past one-night stands and the more casual kind of relationships, they're not really getting to explore that really deep, emotional intimacy that lust can turn into.'

But even when a BRO does manage to have success on the dating scene and get to the point where they can start to get to know a little bit more about their new partner, their living arrangements present further challenges. One of the less apparent side-effects is the extra cost that people in this situation – be they live-at-homers or house-sharers – incur while on the dating scene. More than a third of respondents to the Bumble survey said their situation made dating more expensive because they felt the need to get out of the house more often than would otherwise be the case. After all, a home-cooked meal might be just the kind of romantic gesture that seals the deal for a dater – but it loses some of its sheen when mam and dad are watching *Ireland's Fittest Family* in the next room.

And so, the pool of date-night options is narrowed, and there's a greater reliance on the (increasingly expensive) pub, restaurant, cinema or other activity. One barman I spoke to told me that his mid-week regulars include two house-sharing couples who have clearly established a Free Gaff Rota. One couple comes to the pub for dinner and a pint on a Tuesday, letting the other have the run of the house for a few hours, and then the favour is returned the following night. Two daters I spoke to – who both currently live with their respective parents – told me they simply do not see as much of each other as they would otherwise because doing so would impact on their ability to save for a place of their own.

The need to develop the likes of these inter-couple accords, along with the additional financial burden of dating in the context of tricky living situations, is probably part of the reason why Ellie is not alone in preferring that her prospects have a place of their own. According to the Bumble survey, nearly 40 per cent of respondents said that finding out a potential match was sharing accommodation could be a turn-off for them.

The BROs just can't catch a break.

Obstacle (inter)course

Of course, this is not to suggest that living in your parents' place or in a house share means you're not going to get some. Far from it. The *My World Survey 2* found that 30 per cent of adolescents and 66 per cent of young adults had had sex – because finding any opportunity to do the bauld thing has been an innate skill of the young and horny around the world since the dawn of time.

One living-at-home attendee at the Pitch a Friend event tells me that, in his experience, his housing situation hasn't stopped him dating. Everyone he meets is in the same situation so he's not judged negatively on that basis. But it does make it harder for an initial connection to develop into something more. Another pitchee, Chris, tells me that his parents are fairly understanding of his situation – and sympathetic to the problem it poses to his dating life – so bringing home a girl isn't, technically, a problem. Despite that he still feels the need to take additional precautions when his night has ended well. 'You still need to do the thing where you walk up the stairs in step, so it sounds like there's only one person,' he says.

So, even for the single BROs who are able to get out there, taking a partner home needs to be a carefully choreographed (and footstep-coordinated) affair. And whatever about the smash and grab approach of someone in their early adulthood, the mood music around sex starts to change somewhat as you get well into your mid-20s and, especially, 30s. Those stolen moments in the 10 minutes before your parents get home just start to fall short of ideal. And even if you do match up with someone who's open minded enough to deal with the 'turn off' of you living with your parents, and you have the money to splash out on multiple meals and drinks and activities, there's a point at which a relationship progresses to the point of needing privacy … regularly, ideally.

At this point, do you really want to skulk to your box room like a criminal (or, worse still, a horny teenager) and hope that the bed isn't too squeaky? Or, alternatively, have to drive to a secluded spot and play a game of 'dodge the gear stick'? Probably not.

Instead, you might decide to put your hands in your pocket once again and stump up for a night away. But this doesn't come cheap nowadays – even the most basic hotel room, on the quietest of nights in the tourism off-season, is going to put a dent in your bank balance. Maybe it's no surprise that the term 'love hotel', having not featured much at all in the 2000s and 2010s, is now regularly Googled by Irish people each month. Activity around the search term seems to peak at the start of each year – with 100 searches for it in January 2024. Perhaps all of that extra time with the family at Christmas is what pushes them forward in their hunt.

Love hotels, if you don't know, are a type of hotel that has been popular in places like Japan, South Korea and Hong Kong for decades. Young couples there have faced housing pressures for many years now – so much so that a whole multi-billion-dollar industry developed around the idea that they could book a room by the hour rather than day – although it's not just young couples that make up their clientele …

Now love hotels are something that a relatively small, but growing, number of Irish people are looking for – though so far none exist here. (There's a business start-up idea for you – gratis. No need to thank me.) A kind of middle-ground offering that has come to Ireland, though, is the 'day let' hotel – where a regular hotel offers the use of one of their rooms from morning time until late afternoon or early evening. The attraction for the hotel is that they're making use of rooms that are traditionally empty during those hours.

The hotels that offer this in Ireland tend to pitch them at travellers looking to sleep or freshen up mid-trip, revellers looking for somewhere to get ready for a night out or business people needing a quiet space to take a meeting. The platforms that facilitate these kinds of bookings are less shy about who is within their target market, though, with HotelsByDay.com suggesting a day room could help couples 'reconnect and spice things up'.

But even if this is an option for those looking to relieve the … tension … it's yet another expense. That means it's probably not something the BRO – stuck out of economic necessity – is going to be able to turn to all that often. That means they are facing obstacle after obstacle in terms of getting to have sex and build a relationship, and there's no obvious solution. Except, maybe, opting out altogether.

Cut to the chaste

There does seem to be a significant swing going on in young adults' sexual habits – and not the 'keys in the bowl' kind of swing, either. Quite the opposite, actually. The indicators are that this generation is having less sex than those that have gone before.

The data on this in Ireland is surprisingly thin on the ground. There are some limited stats on when people here tend to lose their virginity and a decent amount of work done on issues around consent, sexual violence and sex education. These are all worthy areas of research, of course, but it seems that, as long as it's involving consenting adults, we don't really want to know any more about what people are getting up to behind closed doors. So, in the absence of Irish information, we need to turn to some international data to get a better picture of this generation's sexual norms – and multiple surveys across multiple countries indicate that Millennials and Gen Zers are having less sex and have had fewer sexual partners than their predecessors.

In the US, for example, a 2019 survey found that around a quarter of under-30s say they have had no sex in the past year. That's roughly double the proportion that said the same thing in a similar survey a decade before. A UK study published in the *British Medical Journal* in the same year found that nearly a third of men and women aged 16 to 44 said they had not had sex in the past month – compared to around a quarter in 2001. Less than half of the respondents said they had had sex at least once in the past week, and there was also a decline in the average number of times 35–44-year-olds said they'd had sex in the past month.

Surveys conducted in Germany, France, Australia and Canada – all of which, broadly speaking, would have similar attitudes towards sex as Ireland – give us similar results. It's led to young adults being dubbed the 'Sexless Generation' as they've reversed the trend of increasing sexual activity that had been in place for many years before.

But why?

In a way this increasing sexlessness would seem counter-intuitive. After all, this is a generation that has a variety of dating apps under its fingertips, making it (theoretically) easier than ever to connect with other singles – be it for a potential relationship or a no-nonsense quickie. But, for many, the dating app revolution has morphed into provoking revulsion remarkably quickly. Like so many other digital social platforms, it started with the promise of improving the way we connect with others but ultimately ended up cheapening the experience. From talking to would-be daters at the Pitch a Friend night, the apps are laden with potential landmines. Some come with the built-in assumption that any resulting connection is a one-and-done kind of thing. And while there's nothing wrong with that, it's also not what a lot of people are looking for.

Even the more 'serious' apps that have tried to circumvent the hook-up culture that has grown up around the likes of Tinder have their fair share of problems too, as Ellie explains to me.

'Obviously you're only seeing the good side of someone, which is probably what you'd want … but as a woman you're then trying to read into the subtext,' she says. 'Okay, he's holding a fish – there's a particular type of guy who does that. In all of his pictures, he's wearing hats – what's going on there? And you end up becoming unnecessarily picky about things that don't actually matter – things that don't correlate to their actual core values or what they're into.'

On top of that, Dr West thinks dating apps have become conduits of a general mood-shift post-pandemic. 'Covid stripped us of a lot of compassion for others because we got so burnt out and fatigued and traumatised,' she says. 'We see it in other areas – like people playing their TikToks at full volume on the bus – and that's translating into dating as well … like sending unsolicited nudes three seconds after you say hello. No wonder people are a bit sick of that – and women in particular are quite sick of that.'

In the end that dynamic is more likely to make for a fairly shallow and isolating experience. Of course, the dating apps still have their place – and have worked for many. But many people, like Ellie, much prefer to meet people in the real world – like at the dating night we're chatting at; it gives people a chance to get a far better, more rounded picture of the individuals they're interacting with. Broadly speaking, in-person dating also somewhat lessens the fears a person may have around being the victim of a scammer or catfisher.

But it's not just the apps that seem to be behind the growing sexlessness among younger adults. This generation has also come of age in an era of unprecedented open-mindedness around sex, with societal sexual attitudes becoming more progressive than ever. Whether that normalisation has made the topic less important to youngsters or there has been a stereotypical occurrence whereby the new generation rebels against the last, a more sexually conservative streak seems to have been sparked within the Bailout Babies.

That's led to the rise of the 'puriteen' movement on social media – young people who are choosing to abstain from sex while also railing against its over-use in TV and film. The depth of this movement is questionable. For every headline proclaiming their impact ('Why are Puriteens mad at Sabrina Carpenter?' – *Junkee*), there are others questioning their social influence ('Are sex-negative "Puriteens" actually taking over the internet?' – *Rolling*

Stone). But there is clearly a detectable shift in attitudes among younger audiences – one that Hollywood at least is responding to. The past decade has been marked by a significant decline in movies rated 18s for sex and nudity, with the industry instead focusing more on sexless (and even romance-less) superhero movies and family-friendly fare like *Avatar*. One of the biggest hits of the past five years was the ultimate icon of asexuality: the literally genital-free *Barbie*.

'In conjunction with the housing crisis you also have a cultural shift with Gen Z. They kind of fall into two camps,' says Dr West. 'One of them is really conservative … a lot of them said they'd vote for Trump, a lot of Gen Z did vote for Trump, and they're watching Trad Wife content on TikTok … and they don't want to see any sex on screen; they're kind of burned out by it.'

As the term 'Trad Wife' suggests, this can manifest in women as an aspiration for a more old-fashioned love life: one made up of fewer partners, little or no sex before marriage (and relatively vanilla stuff afterwards), and clearly defined gender roles within the relationship that see her focus on domesticity instead of a career. At the same time some young men are now expecting this kind of dynamic from a partner – and anyone who refuses to comply is clearly a harlot. Meanwhile one branch of the misogynistic 'manosphere' champions 'Men Going Their Own Way' – with followers rejecting female intimacy altogether due to a belief that women use sex to manipulate and loot from men.

* * *

At the same time, though, others within this generation have gone in completely the opposite direction. 'Whereas the other camp of Gen Z are having the best life – they're identifying with their gender and sexual orientation in new ways and they're having that period where they can explore and ending up in situationships and throuples and polyamorous relationships.'

So maybe part of the dip in sexual activity that has been observed in multiple countries is down to a conservative streak in younger adults. Though if it is, going by what Dr West says, it should at least be somewhat counterbalanced by the cohort that has an extremely liberal attitude towards sex. And even if there is a solid minority of young adults dragging down the average by keeping it in their pants, it would present at most a limited explanation of the overall trend – because the data tends to show that rates of sexual activity are falling even among those who are already in a long-term relationship.

So, are there any other factors that could explain young adults' waning interest in sex? Well, it is possible that some of it is rooted in the economic – and societal – reality of the day.

For a start, some argue that the past data that's being used as a comparison may be misleading us. There is a theory that previous generations of young adults over-reported their sexual activity in older studies in order to make themselves look good. But now, thanks to our more liberal attitude towards sex, the younger people of today don't feel the need to do the same. Or maybe, as we move further and further away from the ideals of the nuclear family, fewer people are feeling the need to pursue intimate relationships at all. After all, it's not just the dreaded dating apps that young adults have under their fingers – they also have just-as-easy access to countless hours of pornography. Surveys both in Ireland and globally have shown the rising use of porn – particularly by young men. It may be worrying to imagine a generation that is replacing real relationships with something digital, but could this explain why sexual activity among men has fallen at a sharper pace than it has among women?

Higher standards of sex education, easier access to information and a growing focus on the self could also be playing a part –

which Dr West says should be seen as a positive. 'People are finding out more about healthy and unhealthy relationships … so, people are pausing and thinking "That doesn't serve me",' she says. 'Maybe in the past they would have been in a relationship that was unhealthy but didn't know what the red flags were. They didn't know what abuse was – they might have only thought it was physical abuse – but now they know there are other forms. People are more empowered now and there's a lot more autonomy, so hopefully a lot more people are waiting for the right kind of situations that make them happy.'

Changes in the broader mood of younger adults could also be playing a part in this trend, too. Some theories suggest that rising rates of depression and anxiety among young adults are having a knock-on effect here, as they (and some of the treatments for it) can dent sex drives and rob people of the motivation to socialise in the first place. But some of the survey data also undermines the argument that a fall in sexual activity is entirely down to a lack of willingness. Results of the UK sex survey show that both men and women say they would like to have more sex than they already do.

So, if people are having less sex than they want to – even when they are in a relationship – then a lack of opportunity surely has to foot a significant portion of the blame. The hectic pace of modern life is contributing to that. Many people are busier, working harder and commuting for longer, which leaves them feeling like they have less time to devote to socialising and, in turn, intimacy. But, as we've already discussed, issues around housing are a problem for young adults around the world at the moment and this is also, unquestionably, a major roadblock for younger people who want to find someone.

But this disjointed dating backdrop – where living arrangements and a lack of money are making it harder for people to find and develop a romantic relationship – is also leading to another side-effect in people's dating behaviours. And it's one that may seem somewhat counterintuitive. On the one hand, the lack of opportunity may have forced some to put their relationship plans on the long finger but, for some who are managing to make romantic connections, it also seems to have led to an acceleration of the courting process.

According to the aforementioned Bumble survey, more than 40 per cent of respondents said they were introducing potential partners to their family earlier than they would otherwise – though that's probably unavoidable if they're all under the same roof. Meanwhile, daters were quicker to talk openly about their finances with their prospective partner, with 21 per cent of 18–24-year-olds discussing salaries and finances within their first few dates.

Daters are becoming less willing to sit back and see how it goes; instead, they want to short-circuit the courting process and work out if what they're dealing with could be a viable relationship – in an economic sense as much as a romantic one – as quickly as possible. This is arguably a reflection of a broader societal trend towards instant gratification and the need for everything, now. But it also represents people taking the cold-eyed, 'fail fast' approach of tech start-ups and applying it to the dating scene. The logic of this is that it improves their chances of only investing serious time, money and emotion into a scenario that has a good chance of letting them fly the nest sooner rather than later.

This accelerated approach to dating, the feeling that dating apps are largely a busted flush, alongside people spending more time at home, makes for a challenging combination in terms of finding 'the one'. And it's led to a growing demand for new ways of connecting with other humans – ones that are very much rooted in the real. The Pitch a Friend event I went along to is a perfect example of that, but in my research I also found plenty of other novel dating opportunities. That included a St Valentine's singles' sauna night, where 12 singles got to know each other while sweating it out in a small, hot room in their underwear. That's undoubtedly one way to speed through some of the early stages of dating. Elsewhere there was an algorithm-powered but real-world matchmaking evening – not to mention the resurgence of the classic (and, for many, dreaded) speed-dating format.

There's plenty of money to be made here, too. A search of upcoming dating nights in Ireland shows a regular stream of tick-eted events – generally priced in the €30–50 range. Personalised matchmaking services, meanwhile, cost a lot more. But clearly people are keen to find 'the one', some as quickly as possible, and so, they're willing to pay good money for even a remote chance of having that happen. And, applying that start-up mindset to it, it can even be seen as a smart investment if this helps get them closer to acquiring a place of their own.

Parental supervision

And so, it seems from all of the above that, having gotten a bad press for the past few decades, long-term commitments are in vogue once again.

'For millennials the biggest fantasy was threesomes,' says Dr West. 'For Gen Z ... the biggest fantasy was monogamy. So, quite a swing in the opposite direction.'

Yes, we went through a period when people realised that finding an adoring wife/husband was not the be-all and end-all and there were more things to strive for in life. And none of those lessons learned have necessarily gone away. But at the same time, for a multitude of reasons, people are craving committed connections once again. That is based on people wanting love but also security and, as unromantic as it may be, even the cold economic realities that used to prompt people – and especially women – to couple up are coming back to the fore in light of today's property pressures.

As a result, the single BROs of this world now find themselves stuck in a negative feedback loop. Living with your parents may make it harder to date, but not dating makes it harder to get out of your parents' box room. It's like a perpetual motion machine that's being sustained by a lacklustre love life. There's definitely the plot to a psychological horror movie in there somewhere.

That's not to say that people will – or should – couple-up purely for the sake of getting their own place to live, but you do wonder if some will lower their standards somewhat 'for the greater good'. Whatever about lowering standards, it's certainly the case that housing affordability is leading some to put up with more from their partner than would previously have been the case. Speaking to one relationship counsellor, I'm told of some cases that they've encountered where people have held on in unsuitable relationships in order to avoid being a Boomerang BRO returning to the family home because they can't afford to go it alone.

The economic reality they face is even going to focus the minds of those who might like to find a partner at some stage but would otherwise have decided it's not all that much of a priority for them at that particular time. Do they hang on and hope – indefinitely – that they'll have better luck on the scene when they're in a place of their own, or do they try to speed up that process by dating now, knowing they may well have to deal with their parents running a fine-tooth comb over everything they do – or don't do – in their search for love.

The government's *Growing Up in Ireland* survey – which has tracked a group from their childhood through to their mid-20s – found that attempts to form or grow a romantic relationship was a common flashpoint between an adult child and their mother. That included rows over sexual behaviour or the child's partner but also rows related to people's social interactions, like them staying out late into the night or their use of money.

It should be said that sex and romantic relationships weren't close to the main sources of disagreement between parents and live-in children – that honour goes to rows about their helping out around the house. Being reminded of how they're falling short in that area probably doesn't sting quite as much as the love-life stuff, but even if it's not directly connected to their attempts at forming a relationship, any friction at home still adds stress to what is already the stressful process of trying to find a mate. It also increases the frustration young adults are feeling – and not just sexual frustration.

A 2023 survey on relationships by media group OneCore found that 91 per cent of couples (of all ages) were content with their relationships. That compares to 81 per cent of single women and 70 per cent of single men.

Granted those figures are still relatively high but that still means that 19–30 per cent of singles are unhappy with their situation, showing just how important an intimate relationship can be in determining someone's overall happiness. It's also worth noting that older people reported being more content than younger people, suggesting that younger single people have the lowest levels of contentment overall.

The survey also found that younger adults tended to see romantic relationships as more important than friendships – perhaps reflecting how the 'quarterlife crisis' makes people focus more on finding a partner than another platonic friend.

Part II

New Pioneers

Social Animals

So, as we've learned, the Bailout Babies have gotten themselves a good education, and they've used that to get a good job that offers them decent – if not amazing – pay. In return, they get to choose between 1) extortionate rents, and pretty much no hope of being able to buy a home of their own, or 2) their parents' box room, a stifled love life and a vanishingly slim hope of being able to buy a home of their own.

But that's not all that's weighing on their ability to date – the financial and time pressures they're under is weighing on all of their relationships. That was particularly true among men. A 2023 survey by OneCore found that 57 per cent of 18–29-year-old males said they hadn't enough time to keep in proper touch with friends, with that number only falling slightly among 30–44-year-olds.

It doesn't help that the avenues for forming new relationships are shrinking, too. The workplace, for example, would traditionally have been a key social outlet for young people, but this generation finds itself at the vanguard of the remote-working movement. A study by Eurofound ranked Ireland second across the entire EU in terms of the amount of time employees spent working from home. That means many of the BROs may not just be living in their parents' box room, they could be spending most of their working days in there too. And remote and hybrid working arrangements also mean that, even when they are in the office, it's half empty. All of this, mixed with factors like longer commute times, means that impromptu work outings have largely become a thing of the past. No number of off-site days, team-building exercises and work-sanctioned fun can make up for that loss.

The other cloud on remote working's silver lining is that it's extending the working day, especially for younger people. Being remote means being more contactable – and in a position to work – at any time of the day or night. And while some may be good at drawing clear boundaries between their working day and their personal time, young adults are far more susceptible to the pressure they may feel from bosses to be on call day and night. Eurofound research shows that younger people are more likely to feel the need to work harder, and respond to their superiors even out of hours, as they seek to prove themselves in their career of choice.

The result of all of this is that young people are finding it harder than ever to form new relationships – not just intimate ones but straightforward friendships too. This narrowing of social outlets – mixed with the ever-growing time pressure from college, work and commuting – means that young adults are increasingly reliant on what you might call friends-by-circumstance for companionship. These are the people they grew up near or went to school with. According to OneCore's study, they represented 70 per cent of respondents' most trusted friend or partner. Meanwhile, just 11 per cent met that important someone through a mutual interest. That's important because a shared love of something – ideally something deeper than memories of going on the mitch – is seen as a vital component in forming a long-lasting friendship.

A consequence of this shift seems to be that young adults are left with a smaller, more distant social network. And all of this combines to leave young adults as the loneliest group in the country – with women aged 18 to 29 and men aged 30 to 44 reporting the highest levels of loneliness overall. In the OneCore survey the loneliness of young men and women ranked far higher even than that of over-60s. That's despite that older cohort traditionally being at the fore of any discussion around isolation in Irish society.

Cut and dry

It would be enough to drive you to drink.

And, in previous generations at least, that would have been the self-medication of choice. After all, the Irish have a reputation for 'dealing' with their problems on the pub stool rather than the therapist's couch. It was once claimed that the father of modern psychotherapy himself, Sigmund Freud, said that the Irish were the only people impervious to psychoanalysis and it's a comment that will ring true for many ... the only snag being that he almost certainly never said such a thing. The claim seems to have originated in Martin Scorsese's 2006 Boston–Irish mobster movie *The Departed* and yet the misquote persists – even finding its way into an essay on psychiatry in the highly respected medical journal *The Lancet*. That's probably because, fabricated as it may be, there is a kernel of truth in there that many of us will identify with. It's believed *The Departed* screenwriter William Monahan possibly got his inspiration for the quote from a comment made by a follower of Freud, who said that human psychology could be separated into two camps: Irish and non-Irish. Even this will be seen as fair comment by many.

Pubs have been at the cornerstone of Ireland's mental-health strategy since the early days of Strongbow (the English earl, not the cider) but they've been at the heart of the country's social scene too. Depending on who you believe, the Irish pub has been a thing for at least 1,100 years – and, in most of the time since, our love affair with the boozer has only grown. In our more recent history, only the local church has rivalled the pub's place at the epicentre of Irish life. Pubs have been the local hub for people looking to catch up of an evening, a gathering spot for those seeking to mark a major milestone or a platform to blow off the stress of a hard day's, or week's, work.

And they have been of particular importance for young people during that time, too. The pub has been the place where people sought to strike out and declare themselves adults. Sneaking off for a few cans was one thing, but the first time you got served at the bar was a whole other achievement. And it was the place where young people could develop their friendships (and other relationships) beyond the schoolyard or deepen the bonds that had been established on the soccer, rugby or GAA pitch. But it was in the weekend blow-out (or blow-outs) that pubs have arguably offered the biggest prize – because over the years, so many people would have built their week towards those precious few hours when they could let off steam at the bar on a Friday or Saturday evening (or often both). And, in fairness, that's not a practice that would be unique to Ireland. In fact, there's a whole sub-genre of music dedicated to the phenomenon; after all, Loverboy told us long ago how everybody was working for the weekend, Michael Grey couldn't wait for the weekend to begin and Tom Waits spent a whole album searching for the heart of a Saturday night. But whatever their taste in music might have been, for many it was that weekly ritual that made the slog of the working week tolerable (and, in a lot of ways, financially necessary).

But the ritual is dying.

Younger people are abandoning the field altogether, skewing the pub-goer ratio further in favour of the auld fella in almost every pub around the country. Ireland's binge-drinking culture – that habit of working to drink and drinking to forget work – is on the way out. So is Ireland's drinking culture in general, actually. For many years now industry statistics and independent studies have confirmed that Irish people are drinking less – and the change on that front is being led by younger people.

Data from the Drinks Industry Group of Ireland found a near one-third decline in average alcohol consumption levels between 2003 and 2023. Studies by both the Health Research Board and *Growing Up in Ireland* show a sharp fall in alcohol consumption among young teens – which can be a critical indicator of potential problematic drinking in later life. A 2022 study commissioned by drinks lobby group Drink Aware showed lower average levels of weekly alcohol consumption among under 34s than the national average.

It's not that young people aren't drinking at all – far from it. Many still go out, but they almost certainly do so less often than their parents would have at the same age. From my various conversations with people in their 20s and 30s, what would have been a weekly occurrence for previous generations is now more likely to be a bi-weekly or even monthly one. And when they do go out, they drink less than would have been 'normal' in a similar session for those who have gone before them. Some tell me that they might start the night later, or finish earlier, while others say that they often simply skip the drink altogether so that they can drive home at the end of the night. The drinks industry is clearly acutely aware of this shift – explaining why breweries and pubs now have a growing array of non-alcoholic options, as opposed to the old tendency of having (at best) a couple of dusty bottles stuffed at the back of a shelf.

One of the dominant reasons for that shift is this generation's increased awareness around, and prioritising of, health. Bailout Babies put a far greater value on their fitness – both for practical and aesthetic reasons – and they are very much aware of just how bad alcohol can be in that regard. That's not solely down to years of public health messaging, either. They've learned from experience that a night on the tear is not conducive to being at the peak of your powers on the pitch the following day. As a generation wracked with anxiety and depression, there is also a sensible reticence around inviting The Fear in on a regular basis to add fuel to those particular fires. It's a far cry from the old tradition of using drink to bury those feelings, in the naive hope that they would eventually go away (or, failing that, you'd die of liver failure).

At the same time, as we've seen, young people have become more comfortable with doing their socialising elsewhere – including on digital platforms. That goes beyond social media and WhatsApp group chats – with many seeing a night chatting shit over a multiplayer game as the perfect way to keep in touch with friends. For this generation, unlike their grandparents and parents, the pub is no longer the only show in town when it comes to catching up with friends.

Meanwhile more practical constraints are raising the bar on what it takes to get out – with those busier work lives, geographical spread and even emigration making it that bit less convenient for groups to arrange a regular meet-up. The shifting sands of the world mean that the culture of the sneaky post-work pint has also been largely smothered, thanks to the aforementioned rise in hybrid working mixed with a lower corporate tolerance for drunk and/or hungover staff.

But it's not entirely fair to say that young adults are avoiding the pub because they don't see it as worthwhile. Many are doing so because it's simply no longer worth their money.

Bar, none

In 2004, Guinness-maker Diageo added six cents to the price of a pint of stout but promised it would then hold prices steady until at least mid-2005. That promise was met with scorn by Irish publicans, who were facing their second price rise in the space of a year. There was particular irritation at the higher price being charged for a pint in Dublin.

'I accept that costs are higher but you'd want a second mortgage to buy a round of drinks there,' publican Con Dennehy told the *Irish Examiner* at the time.

The price he was referring to was in or around the €4.20 mark. Twenty years on, with Guinness prices passing the €7 threshold in many pubs, it's not so much that people are having to get a second mortgage to buy a round. Now they have to forego the drink altogether to give themselves a chance of being able to get a first one.

As can be clearly seen, the drinks themselves cost a lot more than before, and various legislative changes – all arguably worthy in their own right – mean the days of the dirt-cheap student discount and cheap cans before heading out aren't there to soften the blow for young revellers. At the same time, all of the other costs of a night out have jumped, too. Taxi fares are somewhere in the region of 38 per cent higher compared to 2006. And that assumes you've any money left at all once you grab a sneaky burger after letting out time (the price of a Big Mac has roughly doubled in the same time period – so that's going to require a bit more shrapnel than before too).

By anyone's standards going out – in terms of what that meant for previous generations – has become extremely expensive. And that's a problem for Bailout Babies because, counter to the feckless, reckless financial reputation that they've gained (wasting their money on avo toast etc. etc.), they are, in many ways, more financially prudent than their elders. Not only are they doing the 'right thing' in terms of their education and employment, it's also clear that they're doing the 'right thing' with what they earn from their good jobs, too.

According to a 2024 PTSB *Reflecting Ireland* survey, 84 per cent of 25–34-year-olds were saving money, compared to a national average of 75 per cent. Asked what they would do if they were given €1,000 in the morning, 70 per cent of 18–24-year-olds said they would lodge it in a savings account, compared with 42 per cent of over 55s. And the money going into young adults' savings accounts is earmarked for important things too: 37 per cent were planning to put it towards a car, while 27 per cent had a deposit for a house in their sights; 37 per cent of the same cohort were saving for a rainy day.

So, for the Bailout Babies who are doing their best to save, all while potentially paying over-the-odds in rent, the ever-rising cost of a night in the pub is a luxury they feel they can increasingly do without. In a battle between hangover and homeowner, there is a clear winner.

But that brings us back to a fundamental problem. Because, as unhealthy as our drinking culture may have been – in particular, the boom and bust of the work-drink-work cycle –at least it acted as a pressure valve for people. Having something to look forward to and work towards made their week's hard work more bearable – especially if that week was dominated by a less-than-fulfilling job. And without wanting to get into a Yorkshiremen-style debate about which generation had it worst, the withering of this particular release is happening as the upcoming generation have a lot more to vent about than their dead-end jobs. Their arrested development, their struggles to make connections and the ever-moving goalpost of homeownership are all adding to the sense of frustration and listlessness that can come with early adulthood. Not to mention the fact that their own personal anxieties and worries are being amplified by the constant exposure they have – via their doom-machine smartphone – to all the woes that the world has to offer.

So, if they're not drinking their many sorrows away, what are the Bailout Babies doing with their spare time?

Social insecurity

'Every day is a board games day ... on Wednesday we have creative-writing workshops, Thursday night we do movie screenings, Friday is a crafts day, and then we do sober karaoke ... this room here is used a lot for Dungeons & Dragons ... 50 people have been in this room playing video games.'

This is The Clockwork Door – a gathering spot tucked away on Dublin's Wellington Quay. Behind its Georgian door was a network of rooms that served as everything from co-working spaces, to gaming rooms, escape rooms, kitchen facilities, mini-cinemas and just general hangout spots. The wall in one room was dotted with numerous consoles, with a nest of controller cables snaking their way towards the couch. Another room – with an assortment of chairs and couches – was packed with countless board games and books. It all felt very much like the communal area of a student house, only bigger. Coupled with its unconventional format, The Clockwork Door operated on an equally unconventional 'time-house' business model where people paid based on how much time they spent there but then had free access to all its facilities (including the popcorn and coffee machines). It was intentionally opposite to the regular café model, where people might often pay for a coffee or cake in order to get 'free' access to the space itself. And it was designed to be as inclusive and laid-back as possible, with people free to come and go as they pleased and take part in the scheduled activities – or not. Really the only major house rules were that people don't act the eejit and didn't bring in drink.

Going to a place like this, to play board games and sing sober karaoke with total strangers, may not seem like something that would appeal to the Bailout Babies. Based on what we've learned so far, you've probably painted a picture in your head that would be more akin to a hollowed-out hermit whose whole life revolves around that small room in their parents' house. After all, they don't go to the pub much – or at all. They're dating less. They have less time for their friends. They hardly know their workmates beyond their Teams avatars. But, of course, that's not true. Or not entirely true, anyway. Yes, real-world social interactions have declined among younger people and they find it harder to connect with friends as often as they would like. But just because

Bailout Babies' social lives are different – and they're dodging the old habits that lead them to the door of the pub – that doesn't mean that they're a generation of recluses, either. The Clockwork Door was proof of that.

'It's kind of a neutral space – it's not a bar, it's not a pub, it's not a coffee shop – everyone can just kind of hang out as long as they want,' says Dean, 28, who had been coming to the place regularly for the past few months.

Originally from Kerry, he's been living in Dublin for around seven years and is renting in a house-share situation while working for a big tech company. But The Clockwork Door was a great discovery for him.

'A place like this is really handy because my own house is kind of small, kind of cramped – it's nice to have a third space,' he says. 'At work, no-one wants to be there, at home, people want to be there – but the home is where people want to relax, so it isn't really a place to socialise; you kind of go into your own bunker. But too much of that and you get cabin fever and you get depressed.

'A place like this lets you get out, you get to meet people.'

The decline of an Irish pub has, in the past, often been seen as a harbinger of doom for its surroundings – when there's talk of closure, it's usually seen as the end of the area's social hub too. And while pubs may still matter to some local economies, they clearly don't matter quite so much to young people's social lives.

'I think pubs and stuff like that is kind of dying a little bit – everyone is kind of in their own chamber,' says Dean.

Unfortunately, though, it turns out a booze-free business is just as vulnerable to external economic pressures as a pub. A few months after I visited, The Clockwork Door closed for good. Its departure from Dublin represents a major blow to the capital's social scene, and particularly its sober social scene. Though, the no- and low-alcoholic industry it's exiting is far more diverse than the one it entered almost a decade ago – with places like Third Space and Board in Dublin, and Eco Café in Cork all carrying the baton in its absence.

This all goes to show that, while young adults are busy with work and are trying find ways to curtail their spending, that doesn't mean they are too busy saving to find time to socialise. After all, even the most disciplined person in the world would struggle to live their life as that much of a miser. As far back as the 1600s, James Howell was warning that 'all work and no play makes Jack a dull boy' – and he was right.

It's true that some physical socialising has been replaced by the digital – there's no doubt young people are more digitally dependent than older people (though that's kind of like saying young adults don't listen to as many cassette tapes as their parents). And there may have been a time when we believed the promise of big tech – that digital interactions could not just enhance but even replace their physical equivalent. The fact that it has seen such significant advancements in so little time – with the likes of video chats going from blurred and laggy Skype calls to crystal-clear and high-definition FaceTime links – certainly made that seem possible. Tech's relentless encroachment into our everyday lives even made it seem inevitable.

But the worm has well and truly turned in that regard. People no longer believe the hype. The pandemic may take some of the blame for this – having been forced to go cold turkey on the real world while mainlining electronic encounters has gone a long way to souring us all on the experience. The post-pandemic reality of remote working also means that our devices have become much more of a conduit for work and stress than they ever were before. But the tech itself is probably to blame too, because for all of the convenience it gives us, it also brings a fair helping of hassle. It was, perhaps, a self-selective group but everyone I asked at the Pitch a Friend dating night told me of their despair at 'the apps'.

It seems the more we are forced to spend time online and on-device, the more we want to carve out time away from it.

Far from sitting in their parents' bedroom and brooding about that, young adults are actively creating alternative options for themselves. The post-Covid years have seen an explosion in Ireland's social scene – but far removed from the kinds of things that would previously have been assumed to include. In fact, we've already seen other examples in this book – like pottery painting evenings and axe-throwing clubs, as well as unique dating events.

It's no coincidence that many of these are extremely tactile pastimes – almost old-fashioned and retro – but not in an ironic or to-be-sneered-at way. A little bit of searching will, likely, quickly unearth local meet-ups of board game enthusiasts, knitting and crocheting groups with clever names like 'Chicks with Sticks', storytelling sessions and crafting workshops where people help each other to mend and upcycle their stuff. There are book clubs, cinema groups and watch parties. People meet up to share their love of eating pizza, taking photographs while motorbiking around the country and even collecting Callcards (which, if you're too young to know, were pre-paid cards that could be used instead of coins to pay for calls in a public phone booth).

In a lot of ways this idea of socialising over a shared interest or hobby makes a lot more sense than the randomness of making friends based on whoever lives on the road or who sits next to you at school. And, as we've already learned, research has shown that friendships made through a shared interest tend to be far stronger than those that develop due to circumstance. Having said that, those that like a bit of spontaneity are catered for in this new social order, too, with plenty of meet-ups designed purely to help people find new friends or to have a good chinwag. And, feeding into the frugality that comes with the perpetual deposit saver, many of these activities cost little or nothing to engage in.

'It's nice because you can join in with board games, play with people you wouldn't have spoken to before,' says Dean. 'I like socialising in pubs but it can be a little more difficult.'

And, very much contrary to the old way of doing things, these activities are often more focused on improvement, rather than intoxication. Running clubs and walking groups aren't a new thing, but they're now happening at a scale and level of openness that just wasn't possible in the past. Meanwhile a friend asking if they'd like to go for a walk and talk no longer sets off alarm bells of some impending confession or crisis – it's just a normal thing that people do now.

What all of this points to is an incredible amount of resilience and ingenuity among the Bailout Babies. Going to the pub was *the* way to socialise in Ireland in the not-too-distant past. If you were lucky there might have been a cinema or a bowling alley within a reasonable distance too, but that's about it. But the appeal of such a narrow social scope has worn off – either because it is no longer affordable or no longer interesting enough. Instead of retreating further into their digital cocoons, though, younger adults have constructed an entirely new network of outlets that allow them to explore their interests and hobbies in a way that wasn't possible before.

And it's that same kind of resilience and ingenuity that's seen some of them try to turn those interests and hobbies into cold, hard cash.

Hustlers

Davey Comerford, 28, is covered – from ankle to temple – in tattoos. But when I meet the professional personal trainer, he's rocking one body modification that he did not volunteer for.

'It's not broken, thankfully. Just ligament damage and a sprained ankle,' he tells me, with his strapped-up leg being proof, if any were needed.

That obviously makes the day job a little bit harder for him at the moment. By 'a little bit harder', I mean 'impossible'. But, if there's a silver-lining for him, he now has a lot more time to work on his new side hustle: on top of keeping himself and his clients in shape, lately he's also been working on his vocal strength.

'I can't do my gym job but I can slowly build up a bit more of a foundation through my voice-acting work, I can get my voice acting a bit better – I can do stories so I'm not pushed back with deadlines,' he says.

It should be pointed out from the offset that voice acting wasn't part of Davey's career plan. He's obviously at ease being a digital native – having attracted hundreds of thousands of followers to his TikTok and Instagram through his motivational, informative and often simply funny posts. Despite that, it's only recently that he's become acquainted with the platform that's now occupying so much of his time.

'Starting off not having a clue about voice acting to then being a voice actor on a well-established app was pretty like, what the hell?' says Davey. 'It shows that if you're willing to go into an opportunity knowing it might not work but having the courage to say "I tried it", sometimes that can pay off – and it's paid off for me.'

The platform Davey is becoming more familiar with is Quinn which is, put simply, an audio porn app. That means people can apply to become creators and – once approved – post erotic audio-stories, which paying subscribers can then listen to at their leisure. In some cases, the writer of the story is the narrator; in others the writer teams up with a voice actor like Davey to bring their work to life. Popular stories include 'I Need You', 'Thigh's the Limit' and 'Do As I Say'. And, as those titles might suggest, there's a broad number of erotic sub-genres catered to within its library.

Davey's involvement with Quinn came on the back of a rela-tively innocent post he made, responding to some followers who had asked him to explain the story behind his various tattoos. After posting it, he started getting multiple comments compli-menting his accent.

'A lot of them are American – and we have that everybody loves the Irish accent,' he says. 'But I started wondering what I could do with that, so then I decided to read a poem that had a bit of, like, erotica to it too.' That led to a flood of comments telling him he should apply to Quinn, with some tagging the platform in too.

'I had no idea what that was. I'd never looked into voice acting or anything like that,' he says. 'But Quinn contacted me and were like, "Listen, your voice is amazing. Would you like to do an audition?"'

'So, I did a little audition and, lo and behold, they hired me.'

It may not have been what he expected – or planned for – though he does tell me his day job as a personal trainer requires him to be vocal, positive and motivational. So, maybe he was unwittingly training himself beyond his body's strength and fitness. And as a voice on Quinn, Davey finds himself in esteemed company. Other notable actors on the platform include Ireland's own Andrew Scott, as well as *Grey's Anatomy* alumnus Jesse Williams.

The one big difference for Davey is the fact that, having been living in his own place for a while, the high cost of living saw him become a Boomerang BRO. That means he's having to record his Quinn contributions from a corner of his parents' house (I'm assuming that sets him apart from the likes of Andrew Scott anyway but, given the state of things, you never know). And that living arrangement leads to the obvious question as to whether his line of side hustle has been the source of any tension – or awkward moments – between him and his folks. But he tells me it hasn't been an issue in any way.

'They're my number one supporters,' he says. 'I think they understand and they see me try to go out of my comfort zone, or whatever you want to call it, and they see me try to build up a life for myself and to be comfortable.

'So, they're supportive and they understand that it might lead to a future job.'

He also says that part of the beauty of the work is that he can do it from anywhere – be it his bedroom or a nearby coffee shop – and the ambient noise he surrounds himself with can be part of the experience for the listener. But wherever they're working from – and whoever might be in the next room – Davey, Andrew Jesse and the rest of the Quinn crew are part of a broader trend that's seen erotica enter the everyday.

Erotica has, of course, been a part of the literary scene since before there was such a thing as a literary scene. (It was actually around thousands of years before even paper was a thing – with a Sumerian tablet from around 2030 BC containing the earliest known example of a booty call.) But despite its rich history, until recently the audience for erotic literature has been relatively small and one that tended to seek out new work in hushed tones. Until now.

The four novels (and one novella) of Sarah J. Maas' *A Court of Thorn and Roses* series has appeared on the *New York Times'* bestseller list (some genre pedants categorise the series as romance rather than erotica – but it was certainly steamy enough to warrant bans in multiple US states). Rebecca Yarros' *Empyrean* series has sold 12 million copies in just two years, with at least two more books (and a television series) still to be released. And the category spans all kinds of genres – though the more popular ones tend to lean towards the mystical.

'I have a script now and it's nearly like *The Lord of the Rings*; it's like fantasy,' Davey says. 'It has to have that erotica part in it, but it has a story with character development.

'The fascination with it is crazy and really cool.'

And contrary to the sexless trend among young audiences – and the puritanical response from film and TV – these kinds of books are being very publicly embraced by audiences. Social media is now full of posts and memes about people's obsession with stories about other-worldly sex involving monsters, fairies and other 'alpha' creatures – with avid readers trawling Instagram comments and specialist subreddits for recommendations on their next read. And, just as the enduring popularity of the printed word has been accompanied recently by a boom in audiobooks, so too has the growth in erotic novels been joined by an explosion in demand for their aural equivalents – ear-otica, if you will. This is what has led Davey into his new venture.

As interesting as young adults' obsession with erotic literature is, it's not what this chapter is about. Davey may be a trendsetter in the genre he's chosen as a starting point for his voice acting, but what's more relevant here is how he represents the increasingly entrepreneurial spirit shown by people in his generation – because Davey is now a side hustler.

The new nixer

As we know, Davey is, first and foremost, a personal trainer, but he is now earning an extra bit of money from his aural exploits. It's not a huge amount at the moment, he tells me, but he's hoping that will grow alongside his portfolio of work. And while he says he will always stay in the fitness game, he has hopes that his voice-acting work will grow too.

'I think the gym is always going to be my life because that was a foundation,' he says. 'But in 10 years' time, I hope to be well-established. My ambition is to voice a video game character. That would kind of be my dream. From starting off doing a hiking video to creating or voicing a video game character would be amazing.'

Of course, just as there's nothing particularly new in telling sexy stories, finding a little earner on top of the day job is a well-worn path, too. In the past people might have called them nixers, odd jobs or work off the books – and they were generally done by people looking to earn a few quid without necessarily letting Revenue know. But while the basic idea seems the same here, there is something a bit different about the modern iteration of the side hustle.

For a start, side hustles are far more accessible to the average person. They are no longer confined to people with a certified skill – like a tradesperson who is opting to do a bit of extra work on the side. Modern technology means the barrier is getting ever lower and cheaper, making new types of work open to pretty much anyone. And that work might not have any direct link to what they do as a day job. Davey is a perfect example of that. While there were erotic audiobooks (or maybe erotic books on tape?) in the past, that output would have been the remit of professional publishers – it was a closed shop to all but a select few. Now, though, the coming together of the smartphone and its app ecosystem, internet connectivity and the ease of capturing quality audio recordings has made it easier for anyone to offer their content to the world – even a personal trainer with no background in literature, audio or voice work – and it's made it far easier for what he produces to be accessed by the wider world.

Erotic voice acting is just one of the countless number of side hustles that have emerged in recent years. Some are focused on selling handmade products or apparel featuring original designs. It is now entirely possible (in theory) to earn a decent income by posting videos to YouTube. Twitch streamers are earning money by playing video games in front of a digital audience. Pro gamers are earning money by playing video games competitively, often in front of a real audience. Simply being able to influence your social-media followers to buy a certain product is now a highly valuable trait.

But side hustles aren't just focused on creators and gamers. There are options to fit every kind of expertise – even those that have the artistic flair of the assistant accountant at a box factory. More grounded side hustles might involve driving or cycling goods from A to B, form-filling or product testing, re-selling clothes or drop-shipping. Some food delivery apps have even made a point of specifically targeting students and young adults when recruiting couriers, citing the flexibility and choose-your-own-hours nature of the role.

And Millennials and Gen Z have embraced the concept of the second – and even third, and fourth – income stream. Various surveys have suggested that around half of all people in these demographics have a side hustle of some description. They've become so common that the Revenue Commissioners have felt the need to regularly remind the public that the income they generate is liable for tax.

As high as this ratio is, though, it probably shouldn't be a surprise. Even putting the issue of money aside for a second, young adults are part of a far more creative (or at least expressive) generation than what's gone before, and they're far less willing to be defined by their soul-sapping office job. Having a side hustle – whether it's a cutting-edge clothing brand or an ultra-niche podcast ranking Central European crisps – can act as an outlet for their personality and sense of self. The bit of money it might make is a nice little bonus.

Of course, we shouldn't dismiss the financial incentive altogether, either, because we know that Bailout Babies are seeing their incomes stagnate – and in some cases slip behind. And that's happening while the cost of living – and in particular, the cost of striking out in a life of their own – seems to be picking up pace all the time. In that context, the allure of anything that can supplement a traditional income – or, who knows, even replace it altogether – is going to be particularly strong. If that can be achieved while doing something that they're genuinely passionate about, well that's about as close to living the dream as you can get.

There are plenty of high-profile examples of people who have managed to combine their talent with technology to turn it into a hobby with some fairly eye-catching earnings. Seán William McLaughlin – aka Jacksepticeye – has reportedly earned upwards of €7.3 million a year on the back of his massively successful YouTube channel. Matty Gilbert – aka Irish Viking – has previously boasted about earning €50,000 a month from the explicit pictures and videos he posts for subscribers on his OnlyFans page. And while these mega earners are outliers, there are still some who have been able to turn their hobby into a healthy living.

'I still kind of have to pinch myself sometimes,' says Abi. 'It's actually a real thing.' Abi was 35 when she and her partner Audrey set up WeirdWatercolours – which sells everything from cards to calendars to mugs to T-shirts with funny Irish-isms and drawings on them. It's perhaps best known for its 'Jesus Christ What a Year' calendars.

Abi used to work in the service industry but did photography on the side, and she had been a renter since she left home for college. Audrey, meanwhile, was working in retail and still living at home while she studied visual design. Then the pandemic hit.

That obviously impacted Abi's job – but it also created the spark that led to a life-changing business for the couple. Locked down together with Covid symptoms, and with Audrey's visual design equipment to hand, they hit upon a novel way to pass the time.

'We started doing videos on Instagram – just doing draw-along videos and people started joining in,' says Abi. 'We called it #drunkdrawing because it was a bit of craic and nobody knew what was happening back then. It was just an evening thing, and then it progressed to people asking when it was going to be on next – and we were just drawing people's requests.'

But that simple bit of distraction started to grow a larger and larger online following, which eventually turned into an online shop, which in turn has grown into a booming business.

'There was no pre-conceptualising a business – it happened out of circumstance, which is amazing and we're really proud of it,' she says.

The shop is a unique blend of eye-catching art and a very Irish-style of acerbic wit and Millennial irreverence. The hook it's found is probably going to be lost in the translation of anything I write, so you're just going to have to take my word for it. Or you can just look online and see the reaction they've gotten. Because, from a standing start, it very quickly began to generate a viral buzz on social media, clocking up sales in Ireland and around the world. And that meant it quickly morphed from a hobby intended to pass the time to a set of full-time jobs for the pair.

'Audrey learned how to build the website with Shopify … she did courses on tax and how to manage that … so now it's sustaining two full-time salaries and we're hoping to possibly hire a seasonal member of staff for this year,' says Abi.

That success has also allowed the couple to break out of the Tenancy Treadmill and get a foot on the property ladder. 'That was never on the cards for me – and then all of a sudden it was,' she says. 'It wasn't a reality until it was.'

But as much talent and originality as the pair have shown through WeirdWatercolours, it's hard to imagine how they might have gotten on – or whether the business would exist at all – if they'd been starting out 20 years ago. Back then there would have been no digital audience for them to serve as a proving ground, and selling products would have meant trying to build relationships with existing retailers – or investing heavily in a store of their own – rather than selling directly online with minimal risk. Their artistic ability and humour would have stood to them in any context but finding the audience that would appreciate that would have been a far steeper climb in the past. It clearly highlights how new technologies and those lower barriers of entry have created entirely new types of work for those who have the talent, a bit of luck and the willingness to put the effort in.

Everyday I'm hustlin'

Effort is an important – but maybe loaded – word here.

Ultimately, side-hustle culture speaks to the get-up-and-go, entrepreneurial spirit of the Bailout Babies. It is about making the most of whatever you have – be it raw talent, knowledge, spare time or a mixture of the three – and converting that into cold, hard cash. But, of course, the reality is not always that simple. Side hustles might offer the theoretical potential for extra income, but actually achieving that is usually much harder than it seems. And while many may still be striving to find the 'hard cash' bit, most would-be hustlers are likely all too familiar with the toxic side of the hustle that is just straight-up cold.

Because the side hustle has become so common amongst this generation that it has, for some, become an identity in its own right. And that has led to a sub-culture that is, at best, an obnoxious bragging contest and, at worst, a dangerous trap for the desperate.

If you search for 'side hustle' on social media you will likely find one of two things – advice on the most lucrative types of side job and admonishment for side hustlers who are not already raking it in. Often those two things are combined into one post. The more insufferable hustle influencers will talk about how they 'rise and grind' – getting up an hour before they go to bed to ensure they've earned five figures by the time the rest of the world has poured itself a bowl of Coco Pops. They talk about all the money they're making from their 'passive income' streams – which are the unicorn of side hustles because they promise to generate money without any effort. And these self-professed entrepreneurs take to social media and podcasts to detail their impossibly busy daily schedule and how everything they do is focused on adding to their net worth.

Their boasts are usually loaded with a hefty dollop of dismissive scorn, too. If you haven't found a way to monetise every single aspect of your life, what are you even doing? Unsurprisingly, a lot of this type of hustle culture is little more than well-dressed bullshit.

For example, tactics like affiliate marketing (getting a small commission for referring customers), drop-shipping (acting as a digital middle man between a customer and a manufacturer) and selling downloadable, digital designs are all often put forward as easy ways to generate passive income online. You just set them up and the money starts pouring in. Now, if you were the suspicious type, you might wonder why these side-hustle influencers would want to be broadcasting such lucrative information to the world. Surely they'd want to keep that golden goose to themselves. And the thing is, what they're telling you is half true. The likes of affiliate marketing and drop-shipping can make you money and they are relatively easy to set up – so much so that thousands, maybe even hundreds of thousands, of other people are already doing the exact same thing. As a result, the other part – the 'money will pour in' part – is on far shakier ground. The reality is that, to even have a remote hope of making any money from these ventures, you will need to put in significant hours of effort (and quite possibly a lot of your own money, too).

As for why they would share this information with the world, they might claim it's because they've found financial freedom and want others to have the same. But the real answer is more likely to be because they're trying go viral on social media, so that they can then leverage that into an income. Essentially, they're trying to make money by building an audience of people trying to make money – it's like a pyramid scheme but one that's built on views and likes rather than investments. Of course, admitting that this is all smoke and mirrors – or admitting the general weaknesses of their side-hustle recommendations – would undermine their whole grift. So, instead, they tell the audience to follow their tips, and if they aren't making serious money in a matter of days, it's because they're simply not trying hard enough.

Spondoolicks spoofers

The term 'passive income' is a relatively new coat of paint on a fairly old idea.

The same idea was summed up by legendary multi-billionaire investor Warren Buffett, who once said, 'If you don't find a way to make money while you sleep, you will work until you die.' And, as smart as he is, it's not like he was the first person to come to that realisation.

But young adults have clearly heeded his advice and made an attempt to follow his lead because they have become increasingly significant players in investment markets in recent years. The World Economic Forum (WEF) says that 70 per cent of retail investors are now aged under 45, a far cry from the image you might have of paunchy old men barking down the phone to their broker in between a few leisurely rounds of golf. And this trend has been fuelled not only by their increased disposable income compared to previous generations but also their desire to make more of that income where they can. And it's come at a time when it has become easier than ever for the novice investor to make their play on global markets. You no longer need to have a broker on speed dial nor do you need to be networking on the golf course to be an investor. You can now just get one of any number of apps on your phone, and you'll be buying and selling shares, betting on Bitcoin, trading derivatives or exercising options within minutes. In fact, you might not even need to download a new app to do all of this – if you already have the likes of a Revolut account, you'll see many of those trading options sitting right next to your walking-around money.

And that's not necessarily a bad thing. A smart investment strategy is a proven way to boost wealth and the average punter having greater access to that should be seen as a positive. But I stress the need for a *smart* strategy; the problem is that many are not.

Because, as well as identifying the jump in young investors, the WEF also found that the financial literacy rate among young people is quite poor. Less than half of young adults in advanced economies were deemed financially literate. (The Irish in general don't exactly paint themselves in glory in this regard – just over half of those surveyed here were deemed to have adequate financial literacy, trailing nearby countries including Germany, the Netherlands and the United Kingdom.) And poor levels of financial literacy, coupled with an increase in access and activity, translates into a growing group of young people putting their money on the line in ways they may not fully understand. A little knowledge may be a dangerous thing but a lack of it could be disastrous when your money is involved.

Clearly more can be done to make Bailout Babies more financially *au fait* – and there have been steps in that direction. In the meantime, young people have been trying to catch up on the cop-on curve, but they're not necessarily educating themselves in the best places. A finding from a Money Advice and Budgeting Service survey found that 40 per cent of young people here get their financial information from social media. Much like investing at all, that's not problematic in and of itself – there are some smart people giving out good financial advice online (although in some cases their advice may be unwittingly unhelpful to us, particularly if it is based on the rules and regulations that are in place in a different country). However, alongside the actual experts, there's no shortage of straight-ups spoofers too. Just like the Rise and Grind types, they might be people who speak with absolute authority about things that they clearly have, at best, a rudimentary grasp of. Or the type who speak with absolute certainty about how people can make money – which is always a red flag in the world of investments. That being said, these kinds of over-confident idiots are probably the least problematic of the dodgy guru genre – because there are also many internet investment experts who actually have an undeclared vested interest in what they are talking about and they're actively trying to dupe their audience for their own financial benefit.

Coining it

Like Chris 'Crypto' Coyne – our Bargain Bin Buffett.

Twenty-something Coyne rocks a Patagonia gilet, pale blue shirt and Turkey Teeth in what is probably best described as City Boy Chic. With a pass in ordinary level Leaving Cert Business, a copy of *The Art of War* and an eToro account in hand, he's declared himself an Insta investment influencer – though it should be said that little of what he posts would constitute investment advice. His feed is full of vague and not-so-humble brags about how his funds are 'mooning' – which, in this case, doesn't mean 'showing its arse', but rather 'dramatically increasing in value'. And this, he tells us, is because he has 'diamondhands' (a willingness to hold onto his assets in the face of volatility) and he likes to BTD (buy the dip – invest more when prices fall). But most of his posts instead focus on the flash cars and beautiful women that he surrounds himself with, usually in some sun-baked resort.

That's key to the grift, though, because it signals to the audience that the financial finesse of our Bargain Bin Buffett has given him access to the finer things in life. And his followers could put themselves on the same path too, if only they were willing to pay for private access to his economic expertise. And of course doing so is a no-brainer, because results are guaranteed!

It should be said that, from time to time, our Bargain Bin Buffett does grant his wider audience a peek behind the crypto-curtain – tipping them off about some obscure cryptocurrency (like ChancerCoin) or stock (like Yokes Inc.) that they should get into on the ground floor. But even this isn't an act of altruism from our investment guru. It's an old-fashioned 'pump and dump', where they buy (or even create) a cheap asset, talk it up so others follow their lead and then sell it off (at an inflated price), leaving others to hold the can when reality sinks in once again. It's a trick as old as stock markets themselves, and we've frequently seen it deployed in the crypto space in recent years, where new coins are 'minted' and promoted widely as 'the next Bitcoin'. Sometimes they come with a big name attached as a promotional draw, helping them secure a rapid spike in their valuation. But within days – or at best weeks – the price has collapsed back to the asset's true value: nothing. But while crypto may be the latest conduit, the kinds of tricks and scams utilised by these 'experts' are just a modern retelling of age-old schemes. The spoofers pretend to have some special, lucrative insight and rely on Fear of Missing Out and foolhardiness to dupe people into handing over their money. Our Bargain Bin Buffett might be letting you in at the property's ground floor, but he's not telling you that it's a bungalow with dodgy foundations. And if (or when) it all goes wrong, it's all your fault for not buying or selling at the right time – and he's disappeared to Abu Dhabi to take more photos of fast cars and beautiful women (both of which, it turns out, are rentals). These are pretty standard tactics in the spoofer's toolbox and they may seen obvious to some, but grifts like these thrive on the desperation and ignorance of the target market. The WEF study shows us that financial ignorance runs high among the Bailout Babies – and we don't need a survey to tell us that financial desperation does too. And research over the years has consistently shown that financial hardship increases a person's tendency to take risks, as they feel they have more to gain and less to lose in any attempt to break free of their income impasse. At the lower end of the scale, this explains why poorer people are far more likely to spend a sizeable portion of their limited disposable income on lotto tickets – even though they know the odds of winning are incredibly small. At the more serious end of the scale, it explains why poorer people are more likely to take a chance in committing petty – and generally not very lucrative – crimes.

And somewhere in the middle of that scale, beyond those who hold out hope for a lotto windfall but below those willing to put their liberty on the line for a bit of extra cash, are those who miss (or simply ignore) the red flags that may exist in any supposed side hustle. It doesn't take a degree in financial fraud to see how our Bargain Bin Buffett might have an ulterior motive to his investment advice, or that the lifestyle he projects on social media may not bear much relationship with reality. But Bailout Babies' desire to boost their income means they are more willing to invest their time – and quite possibly money – in something that has very little chance of offering them a return. And, as they are being told by 'experts' that a failure to profit from these ventures is down to their lack of hustle, they're then more likely to fall into the sunk-cost fallacy of doubling down rather than cutting their losses. As a result, something that had promised to help alleviate the pressure they were feeling can end up contributing significantly to it.

The naked option

Side hustlers can get pulled into this kind of doom spiral with assets other than their money, too. Some are even, literally, putting their bodies on the line.

Sites like OnlyFans and Fansly have gained a lot of press in recent years – often focused on the money some of their biggest earners are said to be raking in. Those at the top of the pile are said to be raking in millions of dollars each month in return for a few explicit pictures and/or videos. Some of the most vocal Irish models have claimed to be earning ten thousand – and even tens of thousands of – euro a week. And if you're not particularly inhibited, and convinced you're sitting on a gold mine, you might be tempted to dip your own toe in the water (foot pictures do particularly well, I'm told).

The clear implication here is that, in return for showing off what God (or perhaps a skilled surgeon) gave you, and luring in subscribers, anyone can get rich quick.

The coverage often skims over the fact that the top, top earners on the likes of OnlyFans are generally people who had a profile before they joined the site – be they exiles from the 'traditional' porn industry like Mia Khalifa or musicians like Cardi B and Iggy Azalea. That makes it far easier for them to draw in a paying audience. The coverage also, usually, fails to mention that those names are in the top 0.1 per cent – or even top 0.01 per cent – of earners on the platform. To be counted in the top 1 per cent of earners, it's estimated that you probably need to be taking in around $6,000 a month. To make the top 10 per cent, you're looking at a monthly OnlyFans income of around $1,000. And, with roughly four million registered creators on there, that means a far less impressive income for the vast, vast majority of people posting. It's estimated that the average OnlyFans model is earning closer to $1,200 per year.

Those that are making decent money have also likely found that it took far more to get there than simply taking pictures and putting them online. For most it requires not just the DIY photo-shoots but also hours of self-promotion – posting thirst traps across social media and Reddit to draw in new users – and responding to paid-for requests for very specific content. And here the sunk-cost fallacy can have a particularly grim twist – because while people may start out on OnlyFans with a clear idea of what they're willing to share and do, those red lines may quickly start to fade when the money doesn't pour in, and they have to justify their initial decision to post anything at all. Sites like these may allow creators to avoid the exploitation of the traditional porn industry but, in the end, they often just end up exploiting themselves.

In researching this book, I did contact multiple Irish OnlyFans models to see if they would talk about their experiences on the platform, given that they represent an interesting example of modern life's hustle culture. But – contrary to what you might expect for someone in their line of (side) work – I found them to be surprisingly shy about the idea of talking publicly. The vast majority of people I contacted simply did not reply to multiple requests and the ones who did declined to go 'on the record'. Privately, though, I found that some models seemed to oscillate between pride and shame about their naked nixer. It's hard to know exactly why that would be – maybe they were having an ongoing internal battle about their life choices, though I do also wonder if their attitude towards the work was based on how much – or how little – they were earning at any given time. Another OnlyFanser – who claimed to enjoy a significant income from the site – seemed somewhat melancholic about the experience nonetheless. The need to play along with some of the explicit messages – and specific requests – they received seemed to be particularly difficult for them to manage.

But even when it comes to more pedestrian side hustles – ones that don't necessarily involve you taking your clothes off for strangers – the gap between expectations and actual earnings can be difficult to come to terms with. And that takes a mental toll as much as a financial one. Hustle culture tells them they can make money from their skills as long as they try hard enough and that can lead people to turn their hobbies into time- and soul-sucking work. And any time they might spend not working, or – God forbid – relaxing, just becomes a fresh source of guilt.

Industry Inc.

None of that is to say that hustle culture is inherently bad or that all such ventures are bound to fail. The somewhat dull truth is that while some will end up investing more time and money than they earn, some will make a small return, some will create tidy little earners and a handful will hit upon something that is life-changingly lucrative. But even for those who do manage to get their side hustle to cross the threshold of 'little earner' into 'fuck-you money', there are still pitfalls a-plenty. Because despite the fact that – for better or worse – e-commerce industry has now been mostly brought under the control of the big business billionaire class, the internet is full of reminders that much of the web can still be a Wild West.

'I went on to Amazon and I could scroll page, after page, after page, after page of our calendar with our logo and our registered business name on it,' says Abi.

The calendar Abi is referring to is the 'Jesus Christ, What a Year' product that I mentioned before. It became a viral hit – and a break-through moment for WeirdWatercolours. If you're not familiar with it, it features our Lord and Saviour, JC himself, in various states of month-specific grace. February, for example, has the son of God holding flowers and a love-heart balloon with 'Ah Jesus Christ, you shouldn't have!' written beneath him. For October, the caption reads 'Jesus Christ, you scared the shite outta me!', next to a sketch of Himself wearing a Scream mask, with a jack-o'-lantern bucket in hand. Its perfect mixture of goofiness, silliness and irreverence – combined with the cultural nods that were immediately apparent to anyone with an Irish bone in their body – made it a viral sensation.

'We sold over 10,000 copies of it at €25 each – so that was a massive jump for us,' says Abi.

The calendar's sales – and the halo effect it had for the entire business – was the thing that allowed Abi and Audrey to go from just putting food on the table to being able to own the roof over their heads – and that was pretty much overnight. But the popularity of the product meant it quickly got attention beyond customers – with copycats lifting their product wholesale and listing it as their own on Amazon, eBay, Temu and beyond.

'To put it mildly, we shat ourselves,' she says. 'To depend on a product the way we depended on that product in particular – to have to depend on it is scary because I know for a fact all of those platforms have millions of dollars to spend on advertising.

'And they're not selling to a Chinese audience; they're selling to our audience.'

Their experience isn't an isolated one, either. There are countless horror stories of small artists and designers finding their work being duplicated by others – with no cut or even credit coming their way. You might be tempted to call it a black market, only these companies operate very much in the open and on supposedly legitimate platforms like Amazon, Etsy and eBay. You could say it's a cottage industry, but it's often done with the efficiency and sophistication of a large-scale business. In some cases, it's even done directly by an actual large-scale business, with major chains like Zara, TopMan, Anthropologie and Bershka all facing separate accusations of stealing independent artists' designs in recent years.

In the case of WeirdWatercolours, tackling the problem required some professional – and expensive – help. Abi says through all of the legal wrangling, she knows for a fact that the thieves made more money from her work than she and Audrey did. And even with legal experts in their corner, it's unlikely that they'll recoup much or really any of what's been taken from them. These kinds of things are a digital whack-a-mole, and the robbers can set up, sell goods, shut down and disappear quicker than the lawyers can respond to them. Think Del Boy selling his knock-off Rolexes at the market stall – ready to fold up his suitcase and peg it when the Old Bill arrive … except in this instance, it's on the internet.

And the shopping platforms that sit in between the copycat and customer aren't much help, either. 'Amazon will never cancel these guys, eBay will never cancel these guys,' says Abi. 'These third-party manufacturing entities need to exist for those corporations to stay as wealthy as they are. That's the long story, short.'

The best that companies like WeirdWatercolours can hope for is that their willingness to pursue the people stealing from them will make thieves less inclined to rip off their products in the future, and they'll favour a path of less resistance instead, though Abi also worries about any reputational damage that may have been done by unwitting shoppers buying a poor-quality knock-off but thinking it was an original. At the same time Abi has tried to make the most of the situation – even though it's caused her no shortage of anxiety behind the scenes.

'I purposefully made a point of making light of it, and it was a real challenge because I couldn't tell everyone I was scared and I was crying myself to sleep worrying about the future of the business,' she says. 'We have a toddler and a new house now – so that was really scary.'

In the end, though, the traumatic experience also came with a silver lining for Abi and Audrey – which she describes as a full circle moment on social media. By sharing and joking about the experience online, she found that many people rowed in to show their support for the business. 'We gained supporters and we gained customers from the fact that those stories were shared. They had never heard of us before,' she says. 'I had people messaging me saying "I'm a new follower and I've just purchased something because of the story alone".'

Davey also has a depth of gratitude for social media – and the side hustle and associated online community it's helped him to build. Social media is full of traps for people looking to find ways to make extra money or invent a new career for themselves. But for all its ills and the risks that it can pose, it's also the lifeblood of the modern hustler.

'If you're willing to go to social media, you never know what can happen,' he says. 'I never went into social media thinking I was going to get anything from it. I started off doing it as a personal hobby because it made me feel good.' And now he's helping to make lots of other people feel good, too.

Near, Far Away

As I chat to Davey and ask him about recording erotica at his parents', he tells me that it's not going to be a challenge for him for much longer. In fact, by the time you read this, he'll probably be in a different place altogether because he's planning to leave for London.

That's where his long-distance girlfriend lives and, having spent an extended period of time as a couple subsisting on video calls and cheap Ryanair return flights, they feel it's getting to be time for them to make the full-time move to life under the one roof (and ideally one that isn't owned by their respective parents). In fact, the bit of money he's been making from Quinn has been set aside to fund the big move.

Davey seems fairly upbeat about the prospect of crossing the Irish Sea and starting a new life with his other half. I suspect his parents will be sorry to see him go – but also happy to get their bit of space back. For me, the fact that Davey is moving away seems like a bit of good fortune, too. I was looking to speak to him about his side hustle but, as I'm also looking to talk to soon-to-be emigrants, he could fit the bill for this chapter too. As it turns out, though, it wasn't really all that much of a coincidence at all. It seems that once you start chatting to Bailout Babies, whatever the context and whatever their situation, talk of emigration is never too far away. In no time at all, I was spoiled for choice when it came to examples.

Remember our pottery-painting duo Joe and Cliona – the couple who were stuck in their respective parents' homes despite both working hard? When we spoke, the prospect of homeown-ership – or even renting here – was not one that they felt was in their immediate or even medium-term future. So, instead, they've been eyeing up their third option. In fact, their plans to move to Australia weren't in any way notional – they were firm and far along. It was just a matter of Cliona finishing college a few months later and then they'd be all but ready to make the move. Easing the process considerably was the fact that, just like so many other people in their cohort, they already had friends over there who had made the trek and made it work. That made it clear to them that it was a viable option.

'It's a living culture rather than a work culture – it's a lifestyle thing,' they tell me. 'The weather is a big thing as well.'

Both Cliona and Joe are excited about the prospect of enjoy-ing a good bit more freedom, as well as the chance to reconnect with friends. And, let's be honest, they also look forward to the high probability that they'll see sunshine for more than one week a year. That being said, they're also not seeing their move as a permanent one. From what they tell me, they're hoping it will be a medium-ish-term thing. Both tell me they're hoping they'll be moving back to Ireland in a couple of years' time. Maybe at that stage they'll even be in a position to buy. Leaving Ireland with the goal of 'saving while sunning' now seems to be a relatively common one.

That being said, they're not exactly swearing an oath on that front. After all, who knows how they'll feel about the move back when they have a few years in Oz behind them – and who knows what they'd be returning to at that stage anyway?

Another coincidental emigrant that I get chatting to is axe-wielding Ben – who'd felt the demise of his last relationship hinged heavily on the stress that came with failed attempts to find a place to rent. He was also eyeing a move to Australia in the coming months. And like Joe and Cliona, he had friends who had already taken the plunge and only had good things to report back. If the idea of moving was already in the back of his mind, seeing that helped to push it towards the front. And when he took an extended trip to Australia to visit his friends – avoiding the bulk of the Irish winter in the process – the question of whether the move was right for him was quickly answered. When we spoke at the Axe Club the wheels of his trip were already in motion – with his overall aim being to get off this island (and onto that hotter, far larger one) before the days here started to shorten once again.

Of course, the story of Ireland's young leaving these shores in search of a better life is not a new one – Cliona and Joe, Ben and Davey are just the latest in a long list of people to leave this island in search of a better life elsewhere. As anyone with even a passing knowledge of Ireland knows, we've a long and generally bleak historical link with emigration, one encapsulated by – but by no means starting with – the Famine. It's estimated that as many as 10 million people have left Ireland in the past 300 or so years, and we've got a global network of tacky pubs (and a generous helping of generational trauma) to prove it.

But while Ireland's emigration experience may be a long and deep one, what's happening now is not really comparable. The Irish emigration story of the mid-2020s is something very different to the earlier emigration story. Historically, our tendency to board the boats and planes has been intrinsically linked to the economic misery that's been experienced here. Of course, you might argue such a link was bound to be found, given the fact that Ireland's history has essentially been one long period of economic misery, punctuated by brief moments of prosperity. It might seem surprising to some, but the truth is that the post-crash austerity years are far closer to our historical norm than the boom. But as relatively brief as they have been, Ireland has had enough of the good times to allow us to clearly identify the link that existed between economics and emigration – and spot the moment when that tie was severed.

Economics and emigration: a (very brief) history

While Irish emigration has been happening for hundreds of years, the CSO can only tell us how many people came to – and left – Ireland from 1951 onwards. From that, though, we know that between 1951 and 1969, a net 569,000 people sought out a new life overseas. (That number would represent around 19.5 per cent of the country's population by the end of the 1960s – not exactly a ringing endorsement for the new-ish republic.)

But while we think of the Celtic Tiger as the time when Ireland's economy grew up, it did have something of a mini-boom in the early 1970s. Or, more accurately, it managed to string together a few years of growth – which was as good as a boom in those days. Having finally moved on from de Valera's misty-eyed, agrarian protectionism, Ireland opened up to multinational investment and the European Economic Community (EEC). As a result, the economy enjoyed solid, positive momentum for most of the decade with growth averaging 4.7 per cent. And – surprise, surprise – that coincided with a reversing of the migration trend that had been seen up to that point. The country enjoyed positive net migration in almost every year of the 1970s, with more than 100,000 more people coming to Ireland than leaving over the course of that decade.

The country's world-weary populace was sure to have been getting a bit uneasy at all of this positive momentum, but luckily for them, it didn't last very long. By the early 1980s, Ireland's growing population meant there were a lot more people looking for work. Unfortunately for them, their job hunts coincided with multiple local and international headwinds – putting pressure on Irish firms and some of the multinationals that had set up shop here. Irish Shipping Ltd hit the wall; Waterford Crystal faltered.

And while EEC membership was broadly a positive, it also meant firms like Fiat and Ford no longer needed to assemble cars here. The economy returned to its gloomy norm, and by 1986, the unemployment rate had hit 17.4 per cent. Once again, the migration figures followed the economy's lead. Over the course of the 1980s a net 185,000 people left the country – more than undoing the gains that had been enjoyed in the 1970s.

Emigration remained the dominant trend into the early 1990s – before the script was flipped once more. The Celtic Tiger was born in 1994 (though its benefits were being felt before it was even given a name), and had well and truly hit its stride by 1996. In this year, Ireland had 8,000 more people coming than going – with the number ramping up considerably from this point on. In total, in the 14 years between 1996 and 2009, 522,000 more people came to Ireland than left.

But, as we know, by 2009 the Celtic Tiger was no more. It had ceased to be, expired, gone to meet its maker. It – and arguably the entire Irish economy at the time – was bereft of life. And, sure enough, our economic status once again set the tone for our emigration figures. Net migration slipped back into the negative – quite sharply – in 2010, with many clearly seeing the arrival of the Troika as their cue to leave. And more followed them in the years after. The shift was so severe that in a mere five years from 2010 to 2014, around 108,000 more people left Ireland than moved here.

All of this is to say that there is a clear correlation between Ireland's economic performance and Irish people's desire to emigrate. When the economy here is in the toilet, people (generally, young people) decide to leave and fewer people are interested in coming here. When the economy is doing well, more people opt to stay where they are and others – including some of our diaspora – come over. And this trend continued beyond the Celtic Tiger and the subsequent crash. Because, of course, by the middle of the 2010s, Ireland was staging a remarkable recovery, with the country's GDP jumping in 2014 before spiking in 2015 (prompting Paul Krugman's Leprechaun Economics diss), allowing us to formally tell the world 'We're back!' Just as before, the migration trends followed the money, with net migration rising once more and (like the economy as a whole) staying in positive territory to this day.

But here's where things get interesting …

Taking a macro-overview of migration only tells us so much – especially when it comes to understanding the decision-making of our young adults. The Celtic Tiger era is a good example of this because we know that the net migration figure was not just a story of fewer Irish people feeling the need to leave or Irish ex-pats being lured back by the boom. Our migration stats during this era were also padded out by a significant number of non-Irish immigrants who had left their own homelands (just like the Irish of old) in search of a better life. And some of the exodus we saw in the bailout years that followed was made up not just of Irish people leaving but one-time immigrants to these shores moving on to other opportunities. Similarly, we know that Ireland's very recent migration statistics are muddied somewhat by a significant influx of people that goes beyond returning Irish or foreign-born economic migrants. The figures from the past few years include the more than 112,000 Ukrainians who sought refuge here following Russia's full-scale invasion of their country and the tens of thousands of international protection applicants who have come here from other countries over a similar period.

Thankfully, though, the CSO did start to provide a more detailed view of our country's migrants from 2006 onwards – including a breakdown by citizenship. That means we can pick out the movements of Irish passport holders and distinguish them from British citizens, Europeans and anyone else coming from further afield. From this we can see that net migration among Irish citizens mostly follows the same trend as the overall figure we've just discussed. There are net outflows during times of economic hardship (for example, 2010–2016) and net inflows during more buoyant periods (like 2006–2009). Similar to (but slightly trailing) the overall figure, net migration among Irish citizens also swings to the positive from 2017 onwards – right up to the early years of the pandemic (the rate of return actually picks up a bit in 2020 and 2021, perhaps representing Irish people's attempts to be closer to home in light of the pandemic).

But after that point, the figures turn back to the negative. Across 2022, 2023 and 2024 combined, there were 7,700 more Irish emigrants leaving Ireland than there were Irish immigrants returning. In 2024, the number of Irish people leaving the country rose to its highest level since the post-crash days. Overall, 7,700 is not a huge number – particularly in the grand scheme of the country's migration patterns through the decades. But it is huge in terms of the bigger picture that it represents. Because – unlike the outflows of the past – this return to emigration is happening at a time when the country's economy is firing on all cylinders. It is happening at a time of full employment, when – on paper at least – there is no shortage of opportunities available to someone living here.

This is new. Be it during the doldrums of Dev's 1950s Ireland, the depressing gloom of the 1980s or the Dead Tiger years, Ireland's emigration story has always been underwritten by a floundering economy. When things went well people stayed here and others came back – until now. For the first time in the history of the state, the migration decisions of Irish people have decoupled themselves from the nation's economic prospects.

Emi-great expectations

'I was almost 29 when I left Ireland,' says Debra, a native Dubliner who left the country around three years ago and now lives in Queensland, Australia. 'I was a bit older, I guess, than what you'd usually think of – it's usually someone in their mid-20s or even early 20s who goes over and then comes back.

'But, to be honest, I wasn't going over to come back. I was actually going over because I found it so difficult to live in Ireland.'

She had studied social care in Tallaght, Dublin, before going on to work in a homeless hostel in Dublin's Liberties, which included shift work. But it was stressful work – not least because of the ever-growing demand for services in recent years. At the same time, she saw no hope of being able to move out and get a place of her own in the near future.

'I guess I just felt like, in terms of housing, there wasn't much of a prospect in Dublin – I was living at my mam's house, and at 29 you're just past all of that and I didn't really see any way of getting out of that in Ireland,' she says. 'That's more or less why I left – just to have a bit more independence – because it doesn't feel natural. It feels like you're stagnant; that's how I felt.

'You get to 27, 28, 29 and it's that sort of feeling of thinking "God, am I going to be here forever?"'

Having decided to emigrate, Debra initially went to Thailand before opting to head to Australia – in part because she was close to ageing-out of being able to apply for its working holiday visa. She initially landed in Melbourne but didn't like it there, opting to move on to Cairns and, ultimately, Brisbane. And she says that, contrary to the picture people might have of life in the sun, her first few months were a bit of a struggle.

'I wasn't prepared at all coming over. You just think "I'll get a job and it will all work out", but it's not easy for you,' she says.

Her brother had travelled ahead of her but despite knowing people there she found it to be an isolating experience, at least at first. There are also requirements tied to visas – like spending some of your time working in some of the country's smaller towns and cities – which many travellers may not be aware of. It's things like these that Debra now helps other Irish people with in her role at the Irish Australian Support Association of Queensland (IASAQ). Now she fields calls and messages from newly minted immigrants who are encountering the kinds of problems she faced and helps to guide them through the process while also giving them a link to the wider Irish community that's living around them.

'I say it all the time – even though it's an English-speaking country, and we drive on the same side of the road, it's a completely different culture,' says Fionnuala, Debra's boss at the IASAQ. 'And it can be a real shock to the system for sure – and the distance becomes very great and the loneliness can set in. There are stages of migration and settling into a new country regardless, and I think that probably hits home as time goes on.'

If her name isn't enough of a clue, Fionnuala is also an Irish emigrant. She's been in Australia for far longer than Debra – though, like Debra, she also left the Emerald Isle during an era of prosperity. Originally from Laois, Fionnuala, her husband and two daughters headed to Australia in 2005.

'It was a bit different then, I suppose. We left because we wanted to – it's not that we had to. We just wanted to experience something different and do something different with our lives. I call it my midlife crisis!'

Though the plan was to return to Ireland after a couple of years ... 20 years later, there's no sign of that happening. But Fionnuala's status as a veteran emigrant – and her work in the Irish support centre – does give us a very clear picture of the recent trend.

'We've noticed it in the last 12 months – the amount of young people that are coming into the country. Ordinarily, most people came to Sydney, maybe Perth and Melbourne – but Brisbane or Queensland were never places to come back in the day.'

The statistics don't tell us much about the age of the people leaving Ireland – but the anecdotal evidence from Fionnuala, and others, suggests that Debra is a part of a new category of Irish diaspora; the Grudging Globetrotter.

Unlike many emigrants that went before, the Grudging Globetrotter isn't a freshly minted adult heading off in search of some good weather and bad choices. They're not looking to blow off steam before they have to start pretending to be sensible. In fact, they hadn't planned on travelling – and had already gotten their adult lives underway in Ireland, or at least tried to. The Grudging Globetrotter is in their early 30s and – unlike the forced emigrants of old – they're leaving behind a country brimming with opportunity. And that's something that they've spent years trying to take advantage of, to little avail. Emigration isn't their only option: it's a last resort in their attempts to build a life of their own. And for many, it's a one-way ticket.

'Before it would have been people in their early 20s for the working holiday visa, but now people are coming over with the intention of staying, and they're a little bit older as well,' says Debra. 'And families are making the transition over too.'

But a lot of them need help adapting to their new way of life.

'Irish people are sunshine crazy and we get it here in massive doses – I mean, you could easily think you're on a holiday continuously … but you're not, because you still have to work, you still have to pay rent or a mortgage, you still have to pay bills,' says Fionnuala.

It does beg the question whether these Grudging Globetrotters are actually going to find it any easier to get ahead in Oz than in Ireland. Housing was a key issue in Australia's recent federal elections, with some parts of the country facing similar shortages to Ireland, as well as spiralling prices. The median house price in the country is considerably higher than Ireland's too, though Fionnuala says that one difference is there's much more regional variation than would be the case here. Workers can find better value if they're willing to live outside of the big cities. At the same time incomes, especially for skilled workers, also tend to be higher.

'If you come here with a good qualification, if you focus and work hard, it's an easy place to get on,' she says.

Part III

Treat Yo'Self

The Little Treat

How far would you go for a bar of chocolate?

For Jordan, 25, and Jessica, 22, the answer is 'at least 110 kilometres'. Although they would argue that, in this case, it's no ordinary bar of chocolate.

They're from Monaghan, but we cross paths in the Sugar Plum Sweetery in Mullingar, Westmeath – a Willy Wonka-inspired shop that's brimming with all sorts of chocolates, jellies and other sweet treats. Jordan and Jessica have made the trek here solely to pick up some Dubai chocolate bars – a concoction of stringy, filo-like pastry drenched in pistachio cream and tahini, and then coated in chocolate. Developed in 2022 by United Arab Emirates chocolate-making power couple Yezen Alani and Sarah Hamouda, it has since become a much-mimicked viral sensation – so much so that, three years later, its Irish equivalent has prompted Jordan and Jessica to make a cross-country trek. And while we're chatting, they're also frantically fielding texts, WhatsApps and Snapchats from friends at home. Word has gotten out that they've travelled to the shop and so requests are pouring in for them to bring extra bars back with them. They came into the shop with the intention of buying three but have ended up buying 16 instead. And, running at a cost of almost €10 a pop, Revolut payments are being demanded upfront. We may just be talking about a few bars of chocolate, but it's being treated as serious business.

You see, this kind of thing is serious business to the Bailout Babies. As we've seen they are working hard and doing their best to save. At the same time, they are foregoing trips to the pub, late nights out and trips abroad – what many would have seen as the rites of passage of youth. And while they are creating new ways to socialise, they're also exposed to new sources of anxiety and stress about their lives. But while the big blow-out night out might have been what young people once built their weeks – and even mental health – around, the young adults of today have designed a new way to self-medicate. It's very much in keeping with the 'everything, now' approach of the modern age – they've replaced the weekly wait for a night out with a real-time personal incentive system.

'Yes, every day,' says Jordan when I ask if she's inclined to treat herself. And what does she get out of it? 'It just puts you in a better mood or something.'

Jordan and her boyfriend are living with her parents. They've converted the garage, so at least they have something approaching their own space, but they're still hoping to buy a place of their own eventually – if costs come down. Optimistically, she reckons she's four years away from that happening. In the meantime, they're saving, and she says she doesn't go out all that much – bar special occasions like birthdays. Aside from the cost, late nights out aren't a great fit for a nurse who works shifts.

So, like a lot of people her age, she's replacing the tavern with the treat.

Rise of the little treat

In a 2011 episode of US sitcom *Parks and Recreation*, characters Donna and Tom celebrate 'Treat Yo'Self Day', a day they set aside each year to buy themselves anything they want: fragrances, massages, mimosas, fine leather goods, Batman costumes – nothing is out of bounds.

It is, they assure us, the best day of the year.

But while their call to 'Treat Yo'Self' has become a rallying cry for many – and a meme that still reverberates to this day – the treat culture that has adopted the phrase in the intervening years is very different to the once-a-year spending spree that's championed by Donna and Tom. In some ways, it is the complete opposite. To be clear, it is still centred around self-gifting – but the approach people have taken with that has been flipped on its head. Before we get to that, though, it's worth thinking about why we self-gift because this isn't a new concept.

In the late 1950s, American psychologist David Premack published his theory on reinforcement. What later became known as the Premack Principle essentially boils down to the idea that people can convince themselves to do something they dislike by promising themselves a reward at the end. In other words, 'Once I tidy up, I'll be able to sit down and relax with a nice cup of tea.'

In his 1961 book *The Meaning of Gifts*, Swiss philosopher Paul Tournier wrote first and foremost about the gifts we give ourselves: 'those which we allow ourselves in order to put ourselves into a better mood before assuming the less agreeable tasks. Then there are those we promise ourselves afterwards, as a reward'. Needless to say, not even these 60-plus-year-old examples could claim to be the fountainhead of the self-gifting movement – they were just capturing a practice that would have been familiar, to a greater or lesser extent, to people from any era. Even Socrates preached self-care (although he was talking more about spiritual improvement than retail therapy).

But forget about those considered to be among the world's greatest ever moral theorists – perhaps it was internet philosopher Trash Jones who, in a 2022 tweet, best summed up the phenomenon.

Trash Jones @jzux - 16/01/2022
me when I have a bad day: I think I deserve a little treat
me when I have a good day: I think I deserve a little treat

And really, whatever the philosophical or psychological grounding and whatever the occasion, the basic story remains the same. Self-treating is something we're all very familiar with. After all, no-one raises an eyebrow when we treat ourselves to a relatively expensive bottle of something at Christmas time. Celebrating a promotion by buying yourself something nice – a new piece of tech, perhaps – is seen as perfectly acceptable behaviour. Buying yourself that new piece of tech as a consolation prize when you miss out on that promotion is perhaps even more understandable (though, given what is clearly a stagnating career, maybe somewhat financially careless).

But the 'Treat Yo'Self' culture that has been created by the Bailout Babies differs fundamentally in its approach when compared to what's come before. It is a unique combination – thrifty, timely and therapeutic.

'It could be that rather than spending a load of money shopping, we'll go for a walk with the dog and then after we get a coffee and a bun or something else at the coffee shop,' says Jordan.

While previous generations might have focused their self-treating around events or set moments in their personal calendar or even specific tasks, young adults now are making them an inherent part of their day. In their personal contract, treats are no longer an added bonus – they're right there in the basic terms and conditions of their lives. But at the same time, they're not necessarily as expensive as the occasional treats of old.

Trendy treats

The Treat-Seeker is a mid-twenties personal trainer from Clonmel, whose shopping habits may seem contradictory to the untrained eye. She's amassed an army of digital devotees through her series of 'bulk on a budget' TikTok posts, giving out tips on ways of turning the contents of Lidl's reduced-to-clear shelf into a low-cal, high-protein lunch. But sitting proudly alongside those prudent posts is a video detailing her long drive to a cutesy artisanal bakery, where she paid silly money for an elaborately decorated doughnut and an iced latte.

But this is not a contradiction.

Because so much of the Treat-Seeker's life is shaped by what she can't do – including splashing out on branded butter while also having any hope of adding to her savings fund that week. But she's only human and can only delay gratification for so long, and so she finds ways of adding in regular little treats to keep her going. And, as they say, if you're going to do it wrong, do it right.

Like so many trends nowadays, Little Treat culture seems to have first found its voice on TikTok.

A March 2022 post from influencer Morgan Venn, tagged with #littletreat and advocating an impromptu ice-cream, came with the message 'idk who needs to hear this, but food isn't just about nourishing your body, sometimes a surprise midday ice cream makes your day sweeter'. It has 4,600 likes.

In July of the same year, yoga teacher Mel Douglas posted a picture of herself eating a doughnut in her car, describing herself as 'a little treat girl to my very core.

'I don't even make myself earn them because I'm practicing believing I'm inherently deserving of my own kindness at all times,' she explains.

And, as tends to happen with these little ripples in the social-media pond, they slowly gain momentum before exploding into a trend. By 2023 the littletreat hashtag had gained millions of views on TikTok and begun to attract the attention of newspaper and magazine feature-writers. Before long, major brands were trying to join the craze with thinly veiled ads for the potential treats they had to offer.

As the name suggests, Little Treat culture is about giving yourself small, regular treats – rather than one big one at a certain point in time – like at the weekend. This treat can take the form of a more-expensive-than-it-needs-to-be coffee or a café-bought cake to go along with your protein-packed, homemade lunch. Or maybe it's deciding to splash out on a taxi home on a rainy day or buying that audiobook that you saw some influencer rave about or taking an extra-long lunch on your work-from-home day. It's ultimately about creating a tiny-but-constant reward system as a means of knocking the edges off your personal frustrations, smoothing out your existential dread and getting yourself through the day. It's almost like micro-dosing dopamine as a cut-price means of mood regulation.

But, as both Mel Douglas' and Morgan Venn's posts also allude to, the culture is also wrapped up in an attempted shift away from what younger generations see as a toxic attitude towards everything from work to dieting. It is ultimately an expression of this generation's emphasis on greater self-care. It is also a response to their enhanced social awareness and daily exposure to the conflict, intolerance, ecological despair and hate that social media offers almost by default.

Given the viral nature of these Treat Seekers, the Sugar Plum Sweetery is perhaps the most fitting place to see it in action. While the business had been doing fairly well since it was established in 2022, it's entered a whole other stratosphere since its take on the Dubai chocolate bar spread across social media.

'It was busy enough [before]; there'd be people coming in for the pick and mix and obviously the shop itself is kind of an experience,' Lucile, 21, tells me. She's a supervisor in Sugar Plum and Wholesome Kitchen, the sister restaurant that's right next door. 'The likes of Paddy's Day is always busy and Mother's Day and things like that.

'But then it was jam packed … it's just a tiny little shop and you can't even fit everyone in it half the time. It was just flying out of the kitchen; we were packing it into boxes and it was just going straight away – it was 24/7.'

Sugar Plum's owners, Dave and Denise, started looking into making their own version of the viral bar in late 2024, travelling to Dubai to try it first-hand. Once they got back to Ireland, they developed their own take on it and put it on the shelves in December.

Then everything went crazy.

In the wake of their bar going viral, long queues of Treat Seekers formed outside the shop before it had even opened each morning, with people travelling from all across the country – as far as Kerry, Cork and Galway – to get their hands on some. At one point, workers were just about getting bars wrapped in the production area behind the shop before they were grabbed by staff and handed out to paying customers at the front. Somewhat fittingly, given the shop's decor and inspiration, the whole thing is very much reminiscent of the part of *Willy Wonka and the Chocolate Factory* when the whole world goes into a frenzy in search of a golden ticket.

Meanwhile those who chose to order online were, at one stage, told to expect a wait of almost three weeks for delivery, as staff struggled to keep up with demand.

'I think that's partially why people were coming down to the shop because they don't want to be waiting,' Lucile says. 'We always keep the shop fully stocked every day – I'd have people ringing me in the morning and asking if we have stock because they're coming from that far away.'

By the time we chat in April, though, things have calmed down a bit. The lead time for online deliveries has fallen to ten days and, as a likely knock-on effect, there are no longer massive queues snaking down the road. That being said, the shop is still busy, and almost every customer I see is adding at least one Dubai bar to their order (or, in some cases, 16 Dubai bars). One of the reasons for this calmer picture is the fact that other companies have finally caught up with the trend and started offering Dubai chocolate of their own. I've also seen Dubai chocolate lattes and Dubai chocolate doughnuts on offer around the place lately. For Sugar Plum, that means a little bit of the exclusivity and novelty has started to wear off, though there is still strong demand for their goods. Perhaps another and bigger reason why things appear less hectic now is down to Sugar Plum significantly scaling up the business to get on top of their orders. Pre-Dubai, the shop would have had three chocolatiers working on products behind the scenes; now it has closer to 14, split across separate shifts to keep the production line moving for most of the day. They've also expanded the kitchen area to accommodate more machinery and packaging space.

Having worked in Sugar Plum (and its sister restaurant next door) since December 2023, Lucile has had a front-row seat in this remarkable shift – from modest to mad – in the space of a few days. Given her age, she also has a front-row seat observing her generation's shifting treating habits and the despair that's fuelling it.

'I know that if I'm studying for the day, I'll be like "Right, I deserve something nice now" and I'll get myself a chocolate bar. It's little things like that,' she says.

'I'd never even dream of getting a house before the age of 35 – like absolutely not. I know with my parents when they first got part-time jobs or when they just finished college one of the first things they did was start saving for [a house]. But for me, anyway, it just feels like it's a hopeless kind of thing to even be dreaming about.

'So, we put our money towards small things, be that clothes or sweet treats – and all that's because we don't think [a home] is close enough to reach.'

Lucile is currently studying commerce in Galway, coming back to her parents' in Westmeath each weekend and working in the sweet shop and its sister restaurant next door. She's also expecting her first child and she, her partner and their baby are set to live at her parents' for the foreseeable future. While they are trying to save, she says she'd be surprised if they had their own place within the next 10 years.

'It's never been a dream and it's never even been a thought that I could by the time I'm 31 – I'd be surprised, to be honest,' she says.

'Me and my partner are trying to save and we are trying to put away the €10 or €20 you have left but it's hard at the same time if you are trying to live, you know what I mean? It's expensive. Even with college accommodation, it's ridiculous; I'm lucky enough that my parents could help me with it.

'So, I think my mam and dad would be happy enough that if I stayed at home for a couple of years and did save, I'm not just throwing it all out on the sweet treats or drinks, because they know it's going to take a bit longer. And I'm lucky that my mam is up for that because another thing my dad was telling me was that, when he turned 18, it was like "Right, so, when are you moving out? When are you buying your house?" Whereas I think our parents know that it's hard for us.'

So, in the meantime, she plans to do what she can in terms of saving while also focusing on the more immediate things in her life. That includes working in the shop and finishing her college course, as well as looking forward to welcoming her little bundle … and perhaps having the odd little treat here and there too.

The cost of living

What this all boils down to is the fact that Treat Seekers do not see the point in denying themselves some of the little luxuries that life has to offer. If getting an expensive bar of chocolate – rather than a cheap one or none at all – is what it takes to make them feel better, then so be it. And they've collectively agreed not to feel guilty about that. They may be disciplined in their work, fitness and even finances, but they don't punish themselves either. Because standing against a backdrop of all of the serious things they have to worry about – from their own financial prospects to the future of the planet – they've realised that life is hard enough as it is without adding to the misery.

Katherine Locke @bibliogato - 05/02/2025
I checked my bank account this morning and the little treats must stop immediately.
　　But unfortunately I also checked the news this morning and the little treats must continue indefinitely.

This may seem like a contradiction in the context of the Bailout Babies' focus on saving and a desire to get a home of their own, but there is a psychological explanation for this that goes beyond a simple You Only Live Once outlook. This is actually a low-level example of the concept of 'compensatory consumer behaviour'. This theorises that people will make purchases in response to a perceived deficit – be it within themselves or the world around them – in order to make themselves feel better. Those purchases often have a greater psychological value than their functional value – meaning they are worth more to the buyer than the money spent. It is part of the reason why people will spend hundreds of euro on a watch that serves the same function as a €20 Casio.

This helps explain why someone who is trying to save money for a mortgage deposit would also be at ease with spending €10 on a bar of chocolate (having incurred the cost and hassle of travelling a long distance to get it). If they'd just wanted a chocolate fix they could have gone to a local newsagent and spent a quarter of that amount – but that's not what it was about. It's just like how all of us with low-level caffeine dependency could easily put a homemade brew in a Thermos at the start of the day, rather than spend €4 on a far smaller cup of joe in a café later on. Sure, you could do that – but that's missing the point of the process.

Because, when your mammy told you that 'Money can't buy you happiness', she should have added 'but money can be exchanged for goods and services that can'. Sure, it doesn't quite roll off the tongue in the same way, but it does reflect a reality that we've all experienced. After all, an expensive coffee doesn't have much functional value – beyond perhaps a slight, short-lived energy boost – but the fact that it can get you through the day is priceless nonetheless.

According to Dr Denis O'Hora, who lectures in consumer psychology at the University of Galway, this treating habit may also be an example of what's called 'delayed discounting'. This is the way we process the value of having something now, compared to the value it might have if we wait.

'We see this pattern in many, many things – this is why people make short-term decisions. Because a small win today is worth more than a big win in three years' time. If you offer someone €10 today or €11 tomorrow – a euro gain is worth waiting for – but if you give people that choice, some will take the €10 now,' he says.

In other words, consumers don't think that saving that extra couple of euro is going to make much of a difference in the longer term – it represents a minuscule advance towards their goal of owning a home and so spending it on something they can enjoy now is worth much more to them.

But even with this kind of emotion-driven consumption, a treating habit can still line up with a consumer's larger goals around building up their savings for a deposit or rainy-day fund. It's like retail therapy but on a micro level.

'I feel I can afford this better than going out for a sit-down meal,' says another patron of the Sugar Plum Sweetery, Claire, who's 28. She's originally from Westmeath but had been living in Dublin until late last year when rental costs got too high. She's now living in her parents' place once again, while her partner is living with his parents and they're both saving in the hope of being able to buy or build their own home in the future.

'We just cut out on the nights out and all of that,' she says. But she still finds space in the budget for treats, like Dubai chocolate bars.

'You get the same enjoyment out of a coffee and a bar of chocolate and a catch-up with friends than like spending €100 on a sit-down dinner,' she says. 'You get the same satisfaction out of it.'

And she's far from being alone in taking this approach. While some may see Little Treat culture – and its reliance on small, regular purchases – as a poor choice for a generation facing all sorts of financial pressures, the chances are it still represents a more prudent approach to consumption than the old-fashioned 'go on a mad one every Saturday night' habit. After all, even one elaborate craft coffee a day will cost you a lot less over the course of the week than a once-weekly night on the tiles. The added bonus is that you'll probably feel a bit better about yourself afterwards – and maybe even have some semblance of a Sunday too.

You can think of it as frugal yet still flaithiúlach.

How these two seemingly disparate consumer trends can sit side by side can be seen clearly in multiple pieces of research. A 2024 PricewaterhouseCoopers (PwC) survey of Irish consumers found that more than a third of 18–34-year-olds were aiming to save up to 10 per cent of their monthly income (below the national average) while a similar proportion were planning on saving 11–12 per cent of their income each month (above the national average). Despite that, younger adults were also more likely to be planning an increase in their spending across the board.

Overall, 36 per cent of 18–34-year-olds were going to spend more on health and beauty in the coming six months, compared to 28 per cent of all adults; 23 per cent were pricing in higher spending on luxury and designer items, compared to 17 per cent for the national average. Meanwhile, 40 per cent of young adults predicted higher spending on clothing and footwear, compared to 32 per cent overall.

How they're able to do this is perhaps explained in part by the BROs who are earning well but handing up a relatively small amount of that to mam and dad. They are most likely of all to be in a position to save a decent amount while still being left with enough walking-around money to indulge in regular treats. But, by definition, Treat-Seekers' spending habits don't have to be bank-breaking – so even those who are renting and saving can find small ways to reward themselves.

A 2024 survey of US consumers by consultancy group McKinsey found that, while people in their 60s and 70s were more likely to splurge on restaurants, bars and travel, those aged 40 or younger were more likely to direct their disposable income towards groceries.

That indicates that this age group cannot afford to splash out on – or justify the relative extravagance of – a restaurant meal and especially not a regular night away. But what they are instead focusing on is picking up some premium products in their weekly shop. It's a trend that really took off during pandemic lockdowns, when the grocery aisle represented the only real outlet for 'luxury' spending. Since then, older people seem to have returned to the restaurant, but younger adults have not.

This threading of the 'frugal yet flaithiúlach' needle is also reflected in under-the-hood trends at the supermarket checkout in recent years. Data from insights and consultancy firm Kantar has shown that, since the start of Russia's invasion of Ukraine and the inflationary spiral it sparked, Irish shoppers have been trying to economise by switching from branded products to supermarket own-brand alternatives.

An Ernst & Young *Future Consumer Index* survey from mid-2024 found that half of consumers were willing to switch to cheaper alternatives and own brands in order to save money, while a third were happy to join a mailing list for discounts and vouchers.

But while they have sought to economise, that doesn't mean that they're looking to live that yellow-pack life – and so, they're increasingly opting for the middle-lane option of going own brand but choosing the supermarket's premium line instead.

This can also be seen in the arrival and high-street expansion of retailers that try to sit in that IKEA sweet spot, promising good-value versions of what are mostly non-essential items. Think the likes of Decathlon, Jysk and The Range. Our desire for little treats is also giving businesses like Insomnia, The Art of Coffee, Esquires, Wendy's, Krispy Kreme and Pret A Manger confidence to expand their respective footprints in the Irish market.

Big little treats

In spite of the evidence we've looked at already, let's not pretend that young adults are restricting themselves entirely to a little coffee here and a fancy brand of crisps there. They are indulging in their fair share of bigger spending too, beyond the daily little treat.

Having long been an American tradition, the 'Black Friday' shopping event has now become deeply embedded in the Irish calendar. The financial crisis can take at least some of the blame for this, as it was after the crash that struggling retailers here embraced it, in an attempt to drum up some badly needed sales.

In turn, Irish consumers eagerly accepted the extra opportunity for a bargain (or the perception of a bargain), with somewhere in the region of €350 million spent in Ireland during Black Friday 2024. At its peak, something like €150,000 was being shelled out per minute by Irish consumers.

And young adults were leading the charge in this.

In a PwC survey conducted ahead of Black Friday last year, more than a quarter of 18–34-year-olds said they would spend more than €500 during the sales event. That compares to 19 per cent of all adults here and 14 per cent of adults globally. But before that feckless and reckless stereotype starts to rear its head again, young adults were also more likely to use the sales event to buy Christmas gifts for their nearest and dearest: 88 per cent of 26–35-year-olds told PwC they were buying Christmas gifts on Black Friday with 12 per cent saying they were going to complete their Christmas shopping on the day. And while it's easy to think of all this spending as personal, isolated and individual (which it is), it also involves a dividend to the state.

In 2024, the Exchequer took in €21.83 billion in VAT alone. That is the total amount received due to the cut the state takes from almost every single consumer purchase in the economy. Compared to the 2019 figure, it is 44.4 per cent higher. That indicates a significant increase in the amount of consumer spending in Ireland over the past five years.

Needless to say, this isn't all down to young adults; it's a team effort by everyone in the country. But while it would be impossible to work out how much of it is down to all the little treats and big little treats purchased by Bailout Babies, it is fair to surmise that they are responsible for a lot of the change. Because even in terms of the basic demographics, they are a significant – and increasingly important – part of the make-up of Ireland. Based on the Census 2022, the Bailout Babies currently represent roughly 27.5 per cent of the country's adult population. And they are almost certainly making up a bigger percentage of our VAT receipts, as this age group tends to punch above their weight in terms of spending, too.

The 18–34-year-old demographic has long been the most sought after by marketers and brands alike, as they are often seen as offering the biggest return on an advertising investment. That's because they are generally earning decent – if not amazing – money, crucially, doing so without all of the associated baggage that tends to attach itself to people over time and acts as a drag on their spending ability (like the burden of a sizeable mortgage or having to feed and dress the kids, which has a habit of getting in the way of trips out and luxury purchases).

A made-up make-up theory

In some ways the Little Treat trend offers a belated consolation prize to those who bought into the Lipstick Effect – an oft-cited economic theory that was never really backed up with concrete evidence.

Coined by Leonard Lauder (of Estée Lauder), it suggested that, in times of economic hardship, people forego expensive luxuries – often by necessity. But rather than cease their unnecessary spending completely, they replace their big luxuries with smaller ones – like good-quality lipstick. Lauder justified his theory with the claim that lipstick sales in the US rose following the September 11 attacks. From this, he proposed the Lipstick Index as a kind of economic indicator.

It was enthusiastically embraced by many – especially financial types who are constantly trying to read the tea leaves of the economy and figure out what is going to happen next. But, despite the desire for the Lipstick Index to be a thing, the multiple studies that have since been done on the theory and multiple attempts to get it to stand up have identified, at best, a tenuous correlation.

A thorough test by *The Economist* in 2009 found no clear link between recessions and lipstick sales – instead, it found that sales tended to rise during good times too. Some now argue that the trend Lauder spotted had more to do with other factors – like demand for specific products on the market at that time – than what was going on in the broader economy.

After the Lipstick Theory was largely discredited, some of the more make-up obsessed economists out there scrambled for a suitable replacement.

One that emerged mid-pandemic was the Mascara Index – which linked consumers' re-emergence from lockdown with a surge in demand for eye-adjacent cosmetics. The theory here was that masks were undermining the need for a full face of make-up, but people still wanted to make the most of what little of their face was on show. And so, they spent big on mascara. Even taking that at face value (no pun intended), it's influenced by a very specific set of circumstances. Thankfully, we don't have regular global pandemics shaping and re-shaping our consumer habits. But even if some make-up-specific indices are unreliable in normal times, there is still a kernel of truth in the case they're making. As counter-productive as it seems, there absolutely is a link between financial hardship and premium products.

During the global recession many retailers went bust in the face of dwindling consumer sales. But it wasn't like people stopped buying things altogether – they just became more discerning in their choices. So, while your average, middle-of-the-road brand suffered, both the Penneys and Versaces of this world actually saw sales increase. In 2010 – with the global economy only starting to shake off the worst of the downturn – the company that owns Louis Vuitton, Moët and Hennessy enjoyed record revenues, with sales of its champagnes doing particularly well. What seemed to be happening was that the consumers who were struggling shifted towards cheaper options, while those who still had money to spend instead sought out quality (and products that told everyone else they still had money to spend).

'You do see that around recessions – typically what we would expect to see is that you only buy what you need, so when you look across sectors, consumer essentials would survive but more frivolous expenses would go in a downward spiral and then recover when people have more money to spend,' says Dr O'Hora. 'But you do often see these little kind of exceptions in those discretionary spends.'

This echoes what David in the Sweet Plum is experiencing. The people who queue at his door want to treat themselves with a bit of chocolate – but they want it to be something a bit more special than what they'd find in their local newsagent.

So, perhaps now multi-billionaire Leonard Lauder can finally feel like he's achieved something, as today's Little Treat culture at least indicates that he was onto something with this theory that consumers will find a way to reward themselves, even when their purse-strings are held tight. It's just that they're maybe more comfortable doing so in the €5–10 price range, than in the €30–40 bracket.

And one thing that drives it today that would not have been much of a factor when the Lipstick Index was first theorised is the performative aspect of this treating habit. Because another thing that makes Little Treat culture different to the self-gifting practices of the past – and the reason why we even know about its existence – is because so much of it is lived out on social media. Some of this is simply down to how trends become trends – people see something on their Instagram or TikTok feed, they like it and so they look to find a way to join in. But in an age when the image you project via social media can be so important, even among peers, Treat Seekers posting about their little treat can also be a shorthand for their values and priorities.

Maybe by posting a reel of you holding a fancy iced coffee you're hoping to signal that you, too, practise self-care. Or maybe you want to announced how disinterested you are in calorie-counting and denying yourself. Perhaps you want to show how you're trying to support local businesses. Or maybe you just want to show off your new nails and reckon a picture of you holding a cup is slightly more demure than posting 'Look at my new nails'.

Needless to say, brands are wise to this too and now place 'Instagram-ability' high on their list of priorities when developing new products. There's a reason why Starbucks' menu has transitioned from a collection of beige-brown milky coffee drinks to a cavalcade of brightly coloured frappes and fruit drinks – many of which have as much in common with coffee as Genghis Khan has in common with Gandhi. We can also blame this trend on the growing prevalence of eye-catching cakes and muffins in cafés that, sadly, look much better than they taste.

So, if little treats can act as a low-level form of self-medication but also help you to advertise your ideal self to the wider world, so much the better.

It's fair to say, though, that the Bailout Babies are not confining their desire for a pick-me-up solely to the little things like cake and coffee or even the not-so-little things like make-up and personal electronics. In fact, their economic malaise is also sending them on a quest for enjoyment and enlightenment beyond 'things' altogether …

Are You Experienced?

Each night, tens of thousands of people gathered together to chant and sing along in unison. Over the course of 149 nights – spread across 51 cities over 21 months – more than ten million people came along to show their love and adoration. It might sound a bit like a cult. For many, it was a religious experience, but at its core, it was very much a capitalist enterprise too.

This, of course, was Taylor Swift's Eras Tour – by far the highest grossing tour of all time. It was also the subject of the highest grossing concert film of all time and holds no less than six Guinness World Records. The tour itself took in more than $2 billion at the box office, while the concert film enjoyed sales of almost $262 million. And those figures don't include the many billions more that fans spent on merch, food, drink, hotels, transport and – of course – bracelets. Nor does it include the unknowable amount made by unscrupulous ticket resellers on the black market because, even though the tickets themselves weren't cheap – in some cases they were downright ludicrous – there was no shortage of demand in any of the places she appeared. That led to some seats changing hands for thousands of euro on the secondary market. But most people you ask will tell you it was worth every penny.

'It was just such a cornerstone pop culture moment, I guess,' says Kristen, who went to not one, not two but three nights of the

Eras Tour. 'It was unlike any concert I've been to before … part of the fun of being a Taylor Swift fan is the opportunity to, like, have a moment with it all. It was just made such a bigger thing that I suppose other fandoms and other people's interests don't get to have that kind of experience.'

I should make clear from the outset that Kristen, 28, did not pay thousands of euro for a ticket. She was able to access tickets on the initial, official sale and so was able to pay face value (though her outlay was increased somewhat by the fact that she got tickets to three shows). Kristen is an out-and-out Swiftie. Originally from Texas and living in Ireland six years now, she has since studied here, gotten a job in media, has herself an Irish fiancé and even has a strong hint of an Irish accent – but, first and foremost, she's a Taylor Swift fan. In fact, Kristen can comfortably call herself an OG Swiftie. Her older sister introduced her to Swift's at-that-time-recently-released debut album and she's stayed in touch with every era ever since, from Tennessee to Tortured Poets.

'So, 2006, I was 10 … so, from 8 to 15 I had posters in my room, I wanted curly hair, I shopped her Walmart collab-collection, all that stuff,' she says. 'I remember looking at her MySpace because she was really active on there … so I go back with it in that way.'

She slipped into a more casual fandom in the years that followed – somewhat ironically, given that it coincided with Swift's meteoric rise to mainstream pop domination. But, Kristen says, her fandom ramped up again from 2020 onwards – and now she's a true believer once more. And having not managed to see her live until that point, she went all out on the Eras Tour – including a trip to London to catch one of the shows there with friends. And they delved deep into the well of Swiftie culture while they were there – far beyond the shows themselves.

'We made our costumes and with this one you do all the friendship bracelets too,' she says. 'We went to the V&A [Victoria & Albert Museum] because they had what they call a storybook trail Taylor Swift Exhibition – and they had a lot of her old cos-tumes and outfits from every era.' In spite of this, she argues that there was nothing strange about the lengths to which she and her fellow Swifties went to maximise their gig experience.

'If you were told, "If you go to London this week every bar is going to have cocktails themed around your special interest, and then also you get to go to this cool exhibition that's only on for this one week, and then at the end of it, you get to gather with everyone that has your specific interest and experience some-thing" – for anyone they would absolutely take that opportunity,' she says.

She's probably right. And we know all too well that she wasn't the only Taylor Tripper who travelled far and wide in search of a special moment.

It's impossible to know exactly how many of the 10.1 million Eras Tour tickets were bought by people travelling long dis-tances – be it cross country or across countries – but it's sure to be a sizeable number. Barclays estimated that the Irish leg of her tour represented a €150-million boost to the economy – which was based on the expectation that each gig-goer was dropping an average of €1,000 on their travel, accommodation, outfits, food, bracelet-making supplies and so on. But as expensive as things have gotten, not many who were coming to the gig from up the road would have been facing that kind of an outlay. Those coming from further afield – even people from other counties who had to stay the night – may not have been far off it, though. And it's likely that a small but wealthy number of gig-goers would have been pushing up the overall average, with spending far in excess of €1,000 per person.

For example, there was the American family that told the *Irish Independent* they had spent $10,000 on their Taylor Trip before they'd even set foot on Irish soil. Or the New York-based journalist Alyssa Shelasky who detailed her Taylor Trip to Ireland in a *Vogue* column, which included stays in The Shelbourne, Dromoland Castle, Cashel Palace and the Cliff House Hotel. She'd have done well to have managed that for under a grand – though maybe she was able to expense some of it?

And while there has been some debate about just how much the Eras Tour generated for the cities it visited, there is no doubt that it was not just a cultural phenomenon but an economic one too. Swift's six shows in Singapore were credited with boosting the city-state's economy by around $300m. The British leg of her tour was blamed for a temporary jump in inflation – as hotels and restaurants bumped up their prices to take advantage of the spike in demand. Swiftonomics, they called it.

Now Taylor Swift is an outlier of sorts. She exists in a whole other universe – not bound by the same rules of culture, finance or physics as the rest of us. There aren't many, or any, artists who could come close to creating a tour that had an equivalent cult-like impact to Eras. However, it does still act as an outsized representation of a broader story among Millennials and Gen Z.

Wildest dreams

Bailout Babies are done with accumulating 'stuff'. Kind of. It's not that they've necessarily forsaken all of their earthly possessions – they're just far more interested in having meaningful, memorable experiences.

A survey by property firm JLL found that both Millennials and Gen Zers valued experiences far more than their older counterparts. They wanted to be able to find more of them in the areas they lived, and they were willing to pay a premium for them too. A 2024 survey by Barclays found that a third of younger people planned to increase their spending on experiences, compared to a quarter of all adults. Meanwhile an Eventbrite report found that younger adults were planning to direct more of their spending towards abstract experiences rather than tangible things. Part of that is down to changes in the nature of consumerism – acquiring the smaller 'things' is far easier now than it was for previous generations. Your parents and grandparents would have had to save hard for months to get even a basic TV set but nowadays someone on the minimum wage might be able to buy one within a week or two. And, so, the physical has become less special.

But, wherever you look, the trend is clear – it's now less about the haves and have-nots, and more about seeing, hearing and doing.

'There has been this drive in experience holidays or bucket-list travel – people looking for unique and immersive experiences over traditional package holidays,' says Jackie Sheehan, sales director at travel specialists Frosch Ireland. 'People are tired of doing traditional holidays and they're looking for a bit more. It's not enough now to just do your three days on the beach – people want to see more and do more. You want to do something that you feel is going to stay with you for life.'

This has seen a growing demand for left-field destinations and out-of-the-ordinary activities, as well as more eco-friendly trips.

Jackie does say that this rise in demand for experiences isn't solely confined to young people – and it has been building for some time. She credits Michael O'Leary and Ryanair with fuelling this trend. However you feel about them, they have created a relatively cheap gateway to so many parts of the world. The rise of low-cost carriers – and their accessibility to consumers – has also been a game-changer, she says, because it means would-be travellers can take control of their travel rather than having to rely on an agent. That's particularly important to the kind of traveller who wants to keep their costs down.

'Younger people are booking and travelling themselves – cheap flights, Airbnb – anybody up to the age of 25, I would think, is doing their own travel – unless they're doing something way outside the norm where they need expert advice,' she says. 'If you're going to Thailand to do a bit of backpacking, is there value in booking through a travel agent? I have to be honest, you're not going to offer that value to the kids travelling really.'

Like with little treats, social media is playing a part here too because consumers' eyes are being opened to the holiday beyond the beach.

'Everybody wants to be Instagramming or putting their pictures online or tagging the hotel – and I don't think that's ever going away, that aspirational piece of what travel is; because it is aspirational.'

And the accessibility of further-flung destinations and more diverse activities has forced travel agents like Jackie to up their game – and bake the promise of epic experiences into everything they offer.

'A package holiday seems more expensive when you can book your Ryanair flight for €20 and your hotel for €100 – so we had to look at how we're going to do this differently. So, you have to then start looking off the beaten track … and you need that destination knowledge,' she says.

Bigger than the whole sky

In the case of Swift's Eras Tour, the gig itself was, of course, just a part – albeit a vital part – of the experience. The lure of the experience also manifested itself in some people travelling long distances – and spending significant sums of money – in order to be at a show. As part of their attempts to get the most out of it, many also bought specific Taylor- (and in some cases even Travis-) themed outfits, while unfathomable hours of effort were put into the creation of countless colourful friendship bracelets, which were then passed around gigs like snuff at a wake. And – showing her uncanny knack for tapping into the cultural zeitgeist – the fact that she peppered her otherwise identical performances with some show-specific moments ensured each night's experience was unique compared to the last – and so, to a true Swiftie, unmissable.

But while she may be the master of creating experiences, she's not the only one to spot the desire among younger adults to have a real-world experience that brings them closer to their favourite art. In fact, it is a growing feature of all types of fandom. For example, the latest season of *Bridgerton* spawned a touring 'ball' that allowed fans of the show to feel like they had been invited along to a high-society banquet, while *Game of Thrones* has led to the creation of one of Ireland's most-visited paid-for tourist attractions. Of course, this trend is not at all confined to the entertainment world, either. Part of the growth of health and wellness is experiential, as people seek out things that make them feel better or more at one with themselves. Part-time teachers, evening classes and YouTube tutorials are in high demand at the moment as people seek to find and develop new skills or hone their hobbies. Whether you're looking to paint pottery, throw axes, taste wine or enjoy afternoon tea, you likely won't have to search too long until you find satisfaction.

This phenomenon is extending all the way to trips abroad – with travel agents telling me that people are now less and less interested in spending two weeks sitting by the pool in a resort. But why? It may make sense that the well-heeled and well-travelled are willing to splash out to find something new, but what's driving that urge among those who are struggling to start their lives?

Well, the housing crisis can certainly take some credit here. Stuck as they are in their BRO limbo or – like Kristen – on the Tenancy Treadmill, they are working hard and saving harder but not feeling like they're getting any closer to hitting the next maturity milestones. And – just as the daily sting of stagnation has created their need for little treats to help take the edge off – as that drags out into months and years, they find themselves searching out something more. They may be waiting for their real lives to begin, but they don't want to see life pass them by in the meantime. And so, they search for meaning in the way they spend their time.

But the lack of their own home also has a less obvious impact on their materialism. Because, through no choice of their own, they don't have as much need for 'stuff'. They're probably not going to be in the market for many large appliances and – let's be honest – they don't have the space for lots of ornaments, picture frames and pieces of furniture. They are Mandatory Minimalists.

'We're also just a bit older,' says Kristen. 'I already have a blender … It's not like I'm fresh out of college and don't have anything for my kitchen.'

This feeling is also coinciding with a time when our relationship with many types of 'stuff' is shifting, which is feeding into the drive for experiences. It is the case that, in many ways, we need less stuff nowadays. Music, videos and even books can be a purely digital experience if you want, and often the media we consume comes to us within a wider stream of content rather than as a result of a specific, conscious purchase on our part. In some instances, that has driven consumers towards even more tangible forms than before – like the vinyl revival and how cookbook sales have boomed despite the widespread availability of recipes online. But it has also made us turn more towards experiences – like concerts and themed events – as a way of connecting with and expressing our fandom. After all, if we don't have an extensive CD collection to show off, how else can we prove to the world that we are a 'Real Fan'?

The value we find in the stuff that we do still need, or want, is also changing, too. 'Physical items have ballooned in price in a different way to travel or experiences,' says Kristen. 'All clothes these days are polyester and like €200 for no reason – but at least the quality of experiences has stayed the same.'

She's even seen this in a shifting culture around weddings. While gift registries are a relatively alien concept to Irish people, they're still the norm in the US. But she tells me couples that do use them are increasingly asking for people to gift them money to cover the cost of different experiences – rather than asking them to buy physical items. (To be honest, this sounds very much like the Irish system of 'cash in a card' but with extra steps.)

It's also no coincidence that these experiences often tend to be communal events, either. As we've already seen, younger people are living busier, more fragmented and more digitally reliant lives than previous generations. Even the music they listen to and the TV they watch is more insular – they're rarely all tuned into the same thing at the same time any more. That creates an obvious attraction to anything that allows them to connect with like-minded people or experience something that helps to remind them that they are not alone.

And, of course, social media has a part to play here, too, because it becomes a place for our young adventurers to catalogue their experiences for others to see. That not only serves the practical purpose of keeping their friends and family in the loop of their lives, but it can also serve as a humble brag for them and their ability to, say, get tickets to a must-see gig … or to tell the world how good a job they did of leaving their ego behind on their recent spiritual retreat. And social media is contributing to experience culture on the other side, too, because it has made us all far more aware of what others are doing with their lives. While in the past it was possible to not go to a gig and never hear anything more about it, nowadays you would be served an immediate, endless stream of content showing you how that thing you missed was the most amazing event that ever took place.

All of this is coalescing around a core memory for the Bailout Babies – one that has super-charged their fear of missing out. Because while the pandemic – and the extended lockdowns and restrictions – left a mark on us all, it had a particularly profound impact on those who were in their late teens, 20s and early 30s at the time. Many of them had only just started to build up their bank of travel and gig-going and socialising experience. Some of them hadn't even gotten a chance to start before the opportunity was taken away from them. And they are very aware of what they missed out on, wanting to make up for it while they can.

This is me trying

There is a not-unreasonable question to be asked of the Bailout Babies and their love of experiences, though. If they are working hard and saving harder, and doing everything they can to escape their parents' box room or the Tenancy Treadmill, should they really be spending their money – and often a lot of money – on luxuries like gigs, hobby courses and experience holidays?

For Kristen, at least, she feels perfectly justified in her decision. 'I think I actually was in a good place to go at this time,' she says. 'I have my own job. I have my own money for the first time since she's been touring.'

While she is currently renting, she does have one eye on home-ownership in the not-too-distant future. Perhaps more pressingly, though, as we speak, she is just a few months away from getting married. So, it's not like she's lacking in things to set her money aside for. But still, she says the timing was right for her. She is responsible with her money and – even when she did splash out on that trip to see Swift in London – she avoided any *Vogue*-magazine-style largesse in the process (for example, staying in a friend's apartment rather than a five-star hotel).

'So, this was the first time where I could make the decision, personally, to go – and then this tour grew into something bigger then,' she says. 'And I think, whenever the next tour comes about some of that will be back to normal in a way … it wouldn't be to this scale ever again, I don't think.'

Sure, Swift probably has a good few world tours to come, but this one was a once-in-a-lifetime opportunity for the likes of Kristen. She also points out that, given the hype around this tour and the ever-rising cost of everything in general, it's quite possible that the next tour will be even more expensive and even harder to get to than was the case here. In other words, there is no guarantee that she would be in a better situation to go along next time if she'd chosen to sit back and let this tour pass her by.

To Bailout Babies, some of what they hear around their experiential spending is part of a broader chorus of unfounded inter-generational griping. It's based on an assumption that younger people have more money than sense and are inherently reckless. Kristen also feels that some of the commentary and tut-tutting around how much people might spend to go and see artists like Taylor Swift has a faint whiff of sexism to it.

'There's always been such a magnifying glass on things that girls especially enjoy,' says Kristen. 'I'll call out my fiancé directly and say that last year he bought €500 tickets to a soccer match that he didn't go to in the end,' she says. She says that his match ticket cost around the same as her three Taylor Swift tickets.

'That's us two in the exact same situation – his ticket to one football match costing more than my three separate Eras Tour tickets,' she says. 'And no-one bats an eyelid on that … except me, who says to him "What do you mean it's €500?!"'

And as counterintuitive as it may seem, the cost-consciousness of the saving-focused Bailout Baby may in fact itself be a factor in the growth of the desire to do – rather than simply have – more, because when they do decide to spend money, especially on the likes of a holiday, they want to make sure they're getting as much bang for their buck as possible in the process. Just like tighter purse strings can result in people focusing their treat budget on higher quality products, it can do the same for travel plans. If they're going to drop hundreds, or maybe even thousands, of euro on a week or two away, they want to come back with more than just sunburnt arms. They'll at least need some memories and a few unique snaps for the 'Gram as well.

It's worth pointing out, too, that there is a subset within this generation who aren't trying to juggle their house-purchase savings and their desire for an experience-filled life because they've just given up on the former. Time and again I came across people who had given up hope of being able to buy their own place, even in the medium-to-long-term future. In some cases, they had come to that realisation after years of trying to save left them almost as far away from their end goal as they had been on day one. And, at that point, they decided to take that money and spend it on something they could enjoy here and now – like the young family I spoke to who, having saved thousands of euro over the course of two or so years, eventually lost hope and decided it was better spent bringing their kids to Disneyland instead. Or the guy in his late 20s who had taken his would-be deposit and gone backpacking for a year.

That might seem short-sighted and even reckless to some, but it's hard not to empathise with how disheartening it must feel to gain no ground on your goals despite years of struggling and scraping. And you can see why, after trying and failing like that, you might decide to start ticking off the things that you want to do now, rather than wait for some imagined time in the future when you might possibly find yourself better placed to do so.

Think of it as less of a bucket list and more of a 'fuck it' list.

The Kidult Economy

When, back in 2001, American band The White Stripes asked Michel Gondry to make a video for their new single, the French film-maker took inspiration from his son's favourite toy at the time – Lego.

The resulting video for 'Fell in Love with a Girl' was a kind of brick-based stop-motion short film, with (mainly) red, white and blue bricks showing the artists – amongst other things – drumming, singing, running and splashing into water.

Lego, famously protective of their brand, wanted nothing to do with it. When they were approached about supplying bricks for use in the video, they refused, forcing the band to buy thousands of them to complete the project. There's a good chance they would have sued, only for the fact that the patent on Lego's plastic toy bricks had expired by that stage and its branding never appeared in the video. After it was shot, singer Jack White had the idea of including a limited edition White Stripes Lego set with some copies of the single. He approached Lego with this idea but was again rebuffed, with the company telling him 'We don't market our product to people over the age of 12'.

Clearly, though, Lego has had a change of heart since then.

Not only did Jack White claim the company belatedly approached him about collaborating after the success of the video, they also featured the music video on their short-lived Lego Studios website, which encouraged customers to submit home-made movies featuring their Lego sets. More importantly, though, they've also clearly abandoned their 'under 13s only' approach to marketing because, at the time of writing, Lego has 117 sets that are designed for over 13s and another 159 sets that are specifically for over 18s.

Just to be clear, the age designation isn't some kind of film-style categorisation that's warning you about X-rated brick action; it's not like Lego has started making *Fifty Shades of Grey*-themed sets. (I'm sure some committed fan has posted instructions for such a thing online if that's your bag, but Lego itself is still very much a family-friendly affair.) Instead, the 18+ age designation refers to the difficulty – the suggestion being that a child or even young teenager would struggle to build the products in question. And that seems like a fair assessment. Their Eiffel Tower set, for example, has more than 10,000 pieces, with even committed Lego fans reporting a build time of 25–30 hours.

And many of these sets are adult-focused in a different way, too. There probably isn't a huge number of kids wanting to spend hours putting together Earnest Shackleton's *Endurance* or a Leonardo da Vinci flying machine. And the price points are suitably adult, too. Multiple 18+ kits cost upwards of €500, with the full-size Star Wars *Millennium Falcon* currently clock-ing in at €850. It would need to be some confirmation haul for a 12-year-old to manage that.

So really what Lego is doing is tapping into the ever-growing Kidult market.

Kidultery

Kidults are defined as the adults whose consumption habits are more closely aligned with what would traditionally be seen as kid-friendly products. That can be the things they watch – like cartoons – as well as the products they buy – like Lego – and the places they go – like Disneyland. There has, of course, always been an element of the Kidult in the world: the guy who collects comic books in his spare time or the girl who puts a lot of thought into the question 'which Disney princess am I?' But in the past, these types would have been seen as fringe, quirky and maybe even repulsive (think Comic Book Guy from *The Simpsons*). But now, they're very much in the mainstream.

Industry insights firm Circana estimated that the Kidult market was worth €4.5 billion to the European toy market alone in 2023. At a time when toy purchases for actual children are falling – due in part to declining birth rates and the rise of screen-based alternatives – the Kidults are picking up the slack.

There are plenty of theories as to why this is happening.

Once again, the internet and social media are playing a part. While adult Lego and Disney fans have always been a thing, in the past they probably would have remained a relatively quiet part of an adult's personality – perhaps even something they felt they needed to be embarrassed about. If they had a 'childish' fandom, they kept it to themselves while they went about being serious adults in the real world. But the internet has made it much easier for everybody to find their tribe. That isn't always a good thing – it's the same phenomenon that has allowed toxic communities like the neo-misogynist Manosphere movement and the #Thinspo trend that often celebrates eating disorders. But for the most part, its role in Kidultry can be seen as a positive thing, allowing people to proudly share – and build on – the love they have for their quirky hobby. The online world is full of people proudly display-ing their fandom, while it has also made it much easier for people to find and connect with kindred spirits than would have been the case 20 years ago. Suddenly you realise the thing your work colleagues might have been a bit snooty about has become some-thing that would impress a bunch of like-minded people online.

At the same time what would be considered 'kids' entertainment has also risen to meet its new audience, with the sophistication of such content evolving dramatically in the past decade. *Bluey* – the Australian animation about a family of dogs – might be officially aimed at early primary schoolers, but it's been widely praised for its subtle handling of everything from neurodiversity to ageing to infertility. *Adventure Time* may have been a pre-teen-pitched story of a boy and his stretchy talking dog, but over its eight seasons, it tackled weighty issues like grief, puberty and misogyny. For a generation that was, at best, used to seeing a clunky moral message slapped onto the end of an episode of robot horse-riding *BraveStarr*, this may seem like quite a departure. This trend towards 'kids' entertainment that refuses to talk down to its audience is arguably an extension of the increased sophistication seen broadly in TV today. But the fact that it is treating its viewers in this way has also helped bond shows like these to audiences, and allowed them to carry their fandom with them through to their adult lives. It's also made it more acceptable for adults to latch on to these shows and characters – even if they discover them long after they've grown out of the supposed target market.

But even bearing all of those reasons in mind, there's also an underlying psychological factor that has propelled the Kidult market into the mainstream. And it's one that very much ties into the experience of the Bailout Babies.

I personally identify as a Ravenclaw

The rise of the Kidult as a significant economic force was really first articulated in the wake of the Covid-19 pandemic. Stuck at home, with time and money to spare, young adults started spending big on toys and games. Lego Group saw its profits jump by 19 per cent in 2020 and a further 27 per cent in 2021 as millions ordered in sets to keep themselves occupied during lockdowns. Microsoft saw sales in its Xbox gaming division grow by 40 per cent in 2020; Sony saw the amount of time people were spending on their PlayStations rise by nearly 20 per cent compared to 2019.

But it wasn't a coincidence that people directed their time and money towards games and toys like this during the height of the pandemic. They could just as easily have spent it on any number of other products or services – but these categories in particular boomed during lockdowns because they offered comfort and distraction from the grim reality of the world. Much like the way people revert to their younger selves when they find themselves in an old environment, they do the same when they find themselves in need of relief from whatever it is that's causing them stress or anxiety. It's reminiscent of what happened in Japan in the early 90s, when a financial crisis sparked a boom in demand for anime and manga, and cosplay (short for costume play – where people dress up as their favourite fictional characters for fun) entered the mainstream.

And that's what's happening in a bigger way with Generation Bart. In the same way that their living arrangements mean they are stuck in perpetual adolescence, so too are their consumption habits. Facing the frustration of being unable to proceed with their lives, they are seeking solace in the kinds of things that have always made them happy. It's a kind of cultural coping mechanism.

Defining yourself by the things you like – and, more importantly, don't like – isn't new. In fact, it's a bit of a rite of passage during teenage years. Making a statement about who you are by the way you dress is par for the course. But, normally, as people move into adulthood they tend to shift away from that. Their favourite band might still be a part of them, but they suddenly find themselves defining themselves by other things – like their job or where they live or by the fact that they have kids. For a generation that is not being allowed to tick so many of those 'normal' adult boxes, though, the young people of today are seeking out new ways to define themselves – or, in some cases, they've just doubled down on the things that defined them as a teen. On more than one occasion, I've heard people – adults with normal jobs, lives and responsibilities – having earnest, in-depth conversations about which of the four Hogwarts houses they reckon they belong to.

While this phenomenon is being fuelled by a negative experience, that's not to say that it's entirely negative or unhealthy. In some ways, it's the complete opposite. Arguably, what the trend signals is that this is a generation more in touch with their 'inner child' than any that have come before. Sure, that's – to some degree at least – out of necessity. They're not acting like 'grown ups', in part because their economic stagnation makes it much harder for them to be able to truly do so. But it's also, in part, because they just don't feel the need to act at all. They don't feel the pressure to completely abandon what might have previously been considered 'childish' interests in order to show they are mature.

'When I became a man, I put away childish things', said Paul in his letter to the Corinthians. But, as C.S. Lewis argued, that should include putting away 'the fear of childishness and the desire to be very grown up'.

Blast from the recent past

What's interesting is how the consumer market has responded to this, because capitalism is nothing if not adaptable. If it's true that only the cockroaches would survive a nuclear holocaust, you can bet it wouldn't take long before they were being encouraged to buy tiny flatscreen TVs and Stanley cups. The market may not be able or willing to provide hard-working young adults with a home of their own, but it can give them plenty of ways in which to express their fandom – for a price.

Remember that this is a, generally, well-earning demographic with a decent amount of disposable income in their back pockets. They are also looking for things to keep their heads above water, with many turning to this kind of comfort consumption as a means of doing that. If they can do so in a way that reaffirms who they are, all the better. So, it should be no surprise to find that many major companies have spotted the trend – and are making it clear that they are only too happy to capitalise on it.

The result is that nostalgia is now much bigger business than it was before. It's traditionally been the preserve of those getting on a bit, who might be only too happy to buy a 40th anniversary edition of a favourite film or buy tickets to an over-the-hill artist who's shuffled into town on their Pension Pot World Tour. But while nostalgia used to be about people thinking of the good old days when they were in their prime, now young people are muscling in on the act too – only they're reminiscing about the good old days *before* they were in their prime.

It all means that the half-life of nostalgia is now measured in months rather than decades. There doesn't have to be a zero on the end anymore for an anniversary to be significant – illustrated by the likes of Phoebe Bridgers' fifth anniversary edition release of *Stranger in the Alps* and Chappell Roan's one-year anniversary edition of *Rise and Fall of a Midwest Princess*.

This New Wave Nostalgia can be seen across the commercial spectrum. Lego, once again, has excelled in this space (pun intended) with the likes of its 'Blacktron' set. Part of its 18+ range, the sci-fi styled spaceship is a re-released version of a set which was originally on the market from the late 1980s through to the mid-1990s. In other words, just the kind of thing that a lot of people in their mid-30s probably remember playing with (or coveting). But rather than having to trawl through car boot sales and eBay listings, now they can easily relive their youth – as long as they have €100 to spare. Or the same consumer might be more interested in the Lion Knights castle – also a product of the late 1980s and early 1990s. Customers can bask in the warm glow of those core memories for a mere €400.

But it would be unfair to focus too much on Lego. As good as they are at capitalising on Kidults, they're not the only ones.

The maker of My Little Pony and Transformers, Hasbro, has identified the Kidult market as one of the fastest growing categories in its business, saying over 18s now account for more than 40 per cent of their annual revenue. This has led the company to create a specific website – Hasbro Pulse – which encourages fans to show their interest in (and pre-pay for) some of the toys it's planning to make in the not-too-distant future. Meanwhile, last year, Mattel launched a collectibles side-brand called 'Creations', which has already offered a $690 Hot Wheels set designed by visual artist Daniel Arsham and a $300 Japanese-inspired Skeletor toy. Its Fisher-Price brand recently offered a line of 'Little People' toys based on the beer-drinking, paint-huffing sitcom *It's Always Sunny in Philadelphia*.

And, of course, Mattel also made hay from the massive success of the post-ironic *Barbie* movie, which was pitched squarely at the grown-up Barbie kid – leading to a whole new wave of products and merch. It will be hoping to repeat the trick with an upcoming movie based on 1990s kids' favourite Barney. You might assume this – like the original show – will be pitched at small kids, but the fact that it's being produced by Oscar, Emmy and SAG Award winner Daniel Kaluuya and developed by psychological horror specialist A24 Studios suggests otherwise.

Meanwhile there has been an explosion in collectible product lines, which are often relatively cheap in isolation but an expensive habit for anyone who goes in deep. Pokémon might have been ahead of the curve with its 'Gotta catch 'em all' slogan (and it's very much a player in this space), but it's joined today by the likes of the Bobblehead-esque Funko Pops, creepily cute Labubu dolls and ultra-detailed movie-character figurines. And this differs from the collectible crazes of the past – they're not gamified like Pogs or Magic: The Gathering. Nor is there a false promise of future value, as there was in the Beanie Baby craze of the 1990s. Instead, they are collected for collecting's sake. If they hold any value, it's simply as a token representing a person's love of a specific piece of the culture. After all, nothing says 'I love *Lord of the Rings*' quite like a Gandalf rubber ducky.

Needless to say, retailers are responding to this shift too – with Golden Discs probably the best example of that in Ireland. Once the go-to destination for tapes and CDs, the era of the digital download – and, a short time later, streaming music – looked to be the death knell for the brand. And, sure enough, for a time it seemed to be on the verge of retail irrelevance. But the vinyl revival offered it a lifeline and, in more recent years, it has leaned heavily on serving fandoms – with whole areas of its shops now dedicated to band merch, Funko Pops, cartoon pins and TV-themed mugs. At a time when physical music sales are a fraction of what they were 20 years ago, Golden Discs is opening new stores. It's even being joined by some old rivals, with HMV returning to the Irish high street in 2023 with the same kind of 'merch and music' approach to retail.

But while all of these brands have seized on the Kidult market to a greater or lesser extent, the truth is that they sit in the shadow of the master in monetising nostalgia. This is a company that has, thanks to decades of experience, turned it into a lucrative art form.

I'm talking, of course, about Disney …

'You're dead if you aim only for kids' – Walt Disney

Maybe Disney's approach shouldn't be too much of a surprise. The company has long had a solid reputation for being able to market and merchandise its characters, films and shows to kids – weaponising pester power to generate billions at the box office and toy-shop till. And, even since the days of Walt Disney, it's made a point of trying to appeal to adults too. Or, at least, not irritate or offend them enough that they'd forbid their kids from watching. But perhaps the big difference between the Bailout Babies and their parents, or grandparents, is that their childhoods featured far greater access to Disney content than would have been the case before. The vast majority of this generation had a DVD player at home – maybe even in their own room – and quite possibly access to a near constant stream of Disney content via the kids' channels on their home cable or satellite package. The result? Their Disney indoctrination was super-charged.

In recent years, the tweaks Disney has made to its approach means its marketing machine – while still targeting the upcoming generation of kids – is taking full advantage of the seeds planted in the 1990s and 2000s. It is ageing-up in lock-step with that existing audience. It's the reason why a trip to Penneys will net you everything from a Mickey Mouse weekend bag, to a Stitch phone cover, to adult-sized Bambi jammies. It's why the Disney store can get away with selling €200+ figurines based on decades-old films and €90 backpacks styled on a 1990s cartoon.

But it goes beyond marketing and merchandise – Disney's embracing of the adult fan has spread through the entire organisation. That includes its studio, which is increasingly courting the Kidult market through its major releases. And the ever-declining short life of nostalgia can be seen most clearly here, too. In 2019, Disney released a live-action version of its then 25-year-old classic *The Lion King*, in the express hope that it would tap into the affection its (now grown) fans had for the original. In the process they earned a cool $1.66 billion at the box office. This year it's tried to repeat the trick with *Lilo & Stitch*, though in this case, there's only a 23-year gap between the two releases. Next year, audiences will get a live action *Moana* – just 10 years after the original cartoon was first screened.

Disney has also become more and more welcoming of kid-free visitors to its theme parks. There's even a (not-very-inventive) term for them. 'It's just escapism – it's somewhere to go and escape and not really worry about it,' says 29-year-old Kim, who is an event manager for a chain of hotels. Kim and her 31-year-old fiancé Dave have been together for nine years, and they are kid-free and proud Disney Adults, although Kim says she was the driving force behind their visits to Disneyland, initially at least. 'I was always Disney … Dave was always more Star Wars and Marvel.'

And Kim's connection to Disneyland does go way back – she was seven when she first went to the Paris resort, thanks to her mother's uneasy conscience. 'My parents went to Paris for their wedding anniversary and they went into Disneyland for the day … my poor mother felt so guilty that she went to Disneyland Paris without her three children she came home, booked another trip and brought us four months later,' she says.

Her family went on another four trips over the next few years – with the Disney Channel filling the void between visits – until the regular Disneyland trips came to an end in the mid-2010s, in large part due to the crash. By then, Kim was in her late teens and had every intention of returning as soon as she could. So much so that it became an early talking point between her and Dave when they met on Tinder.

'I was due to go on holidays, which I should have been going on with my ex, but I brought my mam instead,' says Kim. 'And I was texting [Dave] the entire time and I remember being, like, "I'd love to go to Disney again, I really want to go back." And then when we were over there, I randomly got a Disney tattoo, and it just kind of spiralled from there.'

When she got back to Ireland, the two went on their first date. Within months they had booked their first trip to Disneyland Paris, and shortly after that, they were on their way to the Florida resort. So far, they've made five trips together – and it would have been more if the pandemic hadn't disrupted their plans. They have two more trips planned for this year – one to Paris and one to Florida.

So, what's the appeal?

'In my field of work, it's very high frequency. It's numbers all day, every day. It's dealing with very stressful situations,' says Dave, who is a senior sustainability engineer with a prominent engineering firm. 'When you go to a place like Disney, things just feel a little bit carefree. You get to kind of go by the seat of your pants and nearly go off on a whim.

'Not to put too much of a funny term on it, but it just feels a little bit whimsical.'

It's a place where serious grown-ups have permission to act like kids for a little while.

Walt Disney saw the potential of the Kidult long before that particular port was manteau'd. He was fully aware of the need to keep parents interested in his cartoons – even though they were ostensibly for kids – and it's said that his original vision for Disneyland was as a place where adults and children alike could go to have fun and relax. But his successors have taken that vision one step further in more recent years. While Walt imagined a place for adults and kids to go together, a 2024 *New Statesman* piece points out that Disney has been trying to make its resorts – and, in general, its output – more adult-only-friendly since the 1980s. That includes opening a nightclub in Disney World and the creation of adult-only cruises.

It's also part of the reason why it spent a combined $8 billion to acquire both comic-book group Marvel and Star Wars-maker Lucasfilm and then a further $71 billion on the acquisition of 21st Century Fox. Sure, these companies offered the potential for more 'content' for the studio – but it's also no coincidence that they all tended to focus on the kind of edgier content that would appeal to young adults (and especially young adult males) in a way that a Disney princess might not.

The decades of hard work (and cultural indoctrination) seem to be paying off finally for the media behemoth. Marvel and

Star Wars movies represent four of the top-ten highest-grossing movies of all time. Spiderman merch is no longer the preserve of small kids and comic-book guys. Meanwhile a child-free adult in Disneyland, which might have appeared odd to some decades ago, has today become a pretty normal kind of visitor to the Mouse House.

Their money, of course, is just as welcome as that of a with-kids family. The only restriction that applies to the visiting Disney Adult, that isn't in place for younger guests, is that they can't dress up as their favourite character while visiting one of the theme parks – for fear that the kids that are at the park will mistake them for staff. But, needless to say, these visitors are more than welcome to don some bejewelled Mickey Mouse ears and character-themed T-shirts, hoodies and dresses – all of which are available for an (un)reasonable price in the resorts' conveniently located gift shops.

But while Disneyland is, in many ways, a shining beacon of capitalism, it's gotten there by offering lots of people the exact thing that they want. Clearly a trip there represents a compelling proposition to many. For Kim and Dave, part of the attraction is the fact that it caters to any type of holiday they might want on that particularly day – whether it's thrill-seeking on a rollercoaster, indulging in cafés and restaurants, taking in live entertainment or just getting your steps in while doing a bit of sight-seeing. 'So, it's almost an all-in-one … I'd nearly call it a quasi-all-inclusive experience,' says Dave.

The appeal has been so strong that they have continued to make trips there while also saving for a house and, more recently, a wedding. And it seems as though more people are seeing the appeal of that – and the allure of reconnecting with their inner child.

This phenomenon is not just the domain of one type of person. As part of her *New Statesman* feature, Amelia Tait conducted an online survey of self-confessed Disney Adults, in order to try to get a better understanding of just what kind of people they are. Close to three-quarters said they were aged between 24 and 44 years old, while the group was heavily dominated by women. There was a relatively reasonable spread in terms of beliefs – a large minority were Catholic, but a third said they were atheist or agnostic. Close to half said their political views were left-leaning, but 18 per cent described themselves as right wing. A further 10 per cent said they didn't care about politics either way.

And that pointed to the underlying feeling of the group as a whole. Because, when asked why they gravitate towards Disney to such an extent, 81 per cent said, 'It offers an escape from an increasingly troubled world'. They were well aware that their obsession was a way of dealing with the problems they were facing – and seeing – on a day-to-day basis. A whopping 77 per cent of respondents simply said that their Disney fandom made them happy, while 28 per cent said it helped them deal with their mental-health issues.

'The whole point [of Walt Disney's resort plan] was the world is hard, life is shit, come here for a day and kind of forget everything,' says Dave. 'I think that's stood the test of time.'

But while that may have been Disneyland's underlying message for decades, there's a reason why it is suddenly resonating so widely today. In Kim's view, the seeming growth of the Disney Adult – and the Kidult in general – is actually down to a whole mindset shift among younger people, because many of them, who have been frustrated in their various attempts to get on with things, have come to the conclusion that life is too short to worry about what other people think.

'I think partially the reason for the rise of what seems like Disney Adults is just the realisation of "I actually don't care",' she says. '"I don't care what people think of me – I couldn't give a shit."'

'I think during Covid a lot of people realised they'd just lost two years of their lives – "I'm not going to lose any more and I'm going to show people who I actually am and what I like, rather than pretending."'

Part IV

Mind Yourself

Are Ye Well?

I find myself lying on a beach with a group of total strangers. It's a dark, cold and windy February night and a voice is telling me to close my eyes and go to my happy place.

But it's not at all what you think.

I'm here for the full moon drumming ceremony arranged by Ellen from Making Waves, a community-based group in north Dublin that holds regular meditation events – mostly in nature. This evening's event is taking place on Portrane Beach and sees us lie on the sand (well, on a yoga mat on the sand) while Ellen drums a steady rhythm and gently guides us towards relaxation.

I'll be honest, though. Despite her soothing tone, the lulling effect of the drum and my repeated attempts to calm my mind, I find it hard to think anything other than wondering, 'Will the feeling ever come back into my fingers?' Checking my weather app afterwards, it tells me it's 5°C out – but the 'feels like' temperature is -4°C. Ellen had warned us to wrap up, and I thought I had – but clearly not enough.

Thankfully, though, the beach meditation is followed up with some time in the nearby sauna. Fears of forever-frozen appendages quickly subside, and I even make a few trips to the plunge pool for good measure. I'm told that it's a relatively quiet night here at the Sea Sauna, but the three cabins seem to be getting plenty of use all the same. Certainly more than you'd expect for a cold Thursday night in mid-February.

But, then again, saunas are having a bit of a moment in Ireland.

Having long been the preserve of some gyms or leisure centres – or a token gesture in the corner of a hotel swimming pool – they now seem to be popping up next to every beach and stretch of coast in the country. Some are being set up in industrial estates and off inner-city side streets. Others are being put on wheels so they can be carted to wherever paying customers might be.

Sitting in a small, hot room in – effectively – your underwear, shoulder-to-sweaty-shoulder with a bunch of strangers probably doesn't seem very Irish. But, 1,200 years after the arrival of the Vikings, perhaps we're finally succumbing to the Scandinavian way of life.

And, if the hour or so that I spent at this particular sauna in Portrane is anything to go by, it seems as though the trend has caught on across age and gender divides. Though while most demographics are represented here, it's fair to say that it skews towards younger adults. But, of course, people's love affair with saunas hasn't sprung out of nowhere. It needs to be seen in the context of a broader trend towards wellness, which has been super-charged by social media and the pandemic.

Wellness Inc.

Wellness, globally, is big business.

The Global Wellness Institute claims the industry was worth $6.32 trillion in 2023 – which would represent a 25 per cent increase on its value pre-pandemic. The institute claims the sector is on course to be worth $9 trillion by 2028.

Now, the Global Wellness Institute has a somewhat vested interest in talking up the prospects of wellness worldwide. As the name suggests, it does act as a representative body for the sector globally. But even if it is making a significant over-estimation in its value – even if it is over-egging the high-protein pudding by 10 or 20 per cent – it would still mean that wellness is a remarkable economic force. If it were a country, wellness would have the third biggest GDP in the world – behind only the US and China.

But if it was a country, it would also be one with extremely ill-defined borders. Contributing significantly to that impressive valuation is the fact that 'wellness' includes a dizzying array of businesses, practices and products. Wellness includes fitness – be it in the gym or with a personal trainer, at HYROX (a fitness class/competition that consists of multiple exercises to give the user a full-body workout) or CrossFit (like HYROX, only more so) or a Pilates, yoga or aerobics session. It includes mindfulness – like meditation, reiki or journalling. It can mean relaxation – like massage or aromatherapy. It is about diet and nutrition – including all manner of health foods, vitamins and supplements. It brushes up against sports and leisure activities. And it includes the already vast beauty industry – and everything in between (and beyond).

Really, it doesn't matter if it's curative, cosmetic or cosmic – what counts in making it qualify as 'wellness' is that it's making the person feel better about themselves.

Of course, it doesn't have to cost money to qualify as 'wellness' – there are plenty of types of exercise or mindfulness that only cost you your time. But, just in case you are ready and able to spend, there are also all manner of products and services that promise to help you on your wellness journey for a nominal charge (or, in many cases, a regular monthly fee). That includes digital goods as much as physical ones – with your smartphone putting you only a tap away from countless apps that claim to help you lose weight, lift heavy, run fast or simply unwind.

Exactly how much all of this is worth in Ireland specifically is hard to figure out. The Global Wellness Industry says per capita spending in Europe in 2023 was $1,596. Taking that figure and applying it to the population here suggests that spending in Ireland would have been in the region of $8.4 billion in the same year.

A pre-pandemic EuropeActive survey suggested health and fitness clubs here were generating €281 million in revenue from their 500,000+ members. But that's reflective of a fairly narrow pool of businesses – it wouldn't include the money made from all the parish hall Pilates and community centre cardio classes that take place up and down the country every day of every week of the year. It certainly wouldn't include the likes of sea saunas and beach meditation, either.

A separate survey conducted by Pure Telecom suggested the average adult was spending €143 a year on fitness tech – including wellness apps and online trackers. Multiplied out, that would represent €500m in spending each year in this category alone.

But while the exact size of the Irish wellness economy is hard to pin down, it is clear that young adults are at its vanguard.

Well, well, well

A 2024 *Future of Wellness* report by global consultancy firm McKinsey found that people in their teens to late 20s had a far greater focus on wellness than their older equivalents. They were spending more than older generations on wellness-related goods and services, with a particular preference for things that promised to improve their appearance or overall health. Though, the survey notes, they were also out-spending older consumers when it came to mindfulness, be that in the form of meditation classes or therapy sessions.

The McKinsey survey was conducted amongst consumers in North America and China and, while there is no equivalent Irish survey, there are various strands of data that would point towards a similar trend here.

Surveys by the state body Sports Ireland have repeatedly shown higher levels of sports participation among younger people through the years. But more recent data shows the figure has reached a new high. Its 2023 survey found that 64 per cent of under 35s were participating in sport – higher than the pre-pandemic figure and comfortably above its 2017 baseline. But it is also well above the participation rate among over 35s, which hit 40 per cent in 2023 (also an improvement on the pre-pandemic figure, it should be said). Younger people were also more likely to be 'highly active'.

Part of that is down to greater knowledge about the various benefits of fitness, but also a feeling among the young that they have a greater need for those dividends because young adults are also feeling more stressed, anxious and depressed than their predecessors. The *My World Survey 2* showed that the majority of 18–24-year-olds had some level of depression or anxiety, with roughly a third in the 'severe' to 'very severe' range (more on this later).

If there is an upside to this, it's that this generation is more aware of their and others' mental and physical health. They also recognise the importance of maintaining good health and are more open to the various techniques and practices that might help achieve that. A 2024 survey by the cross-border Institute of Public Health found a high level of awareness among young adults about the positive impacts that regular exercise can have on a person's physical and mental health. And they were putting that into action, based on the findings of the *My World Survey 2*. It found that 32 per cent of young adults used exercise as one of their top three coping strategies for dealing with problems, with 14 per cent saying they went for a walk as way of managing their mental health.

Intertwined with that is the importance of exercise as a social outlet. As pub meet-ups get less attractive and all the nightclubs close down, sport is becoming the new stomping ground. While the Sport Ireland survey found that younger people leaned heavily towards 'personal exercise', it also showed far higher participation in team-based outlets like football and soccer. It also found that younger adults had better social participation than older people, largely thanks to the clubs that they were members of. Over 35s were more likely to make the bulk of their social contact through volunteering and events.

But, again, wellness is not a one-size-fits-all situation. The *My World Survey 2* also found that 34 per cent used 'taking time out' as one of their key coping strategies for mental health and anxiety – and, if it works for them, that counts just as much as any form of exercise.

On a fundamental level, Bailout Babies are compensating for a lack of control in a major part of their lives by focusing on something they can change. They are prioritising their own health and taking the opportunity to 'work on me'. Whatever their preferred way of doing that, the rising importance of wellness among younger people seems to be the result of a culmination of factors. The growth of the self-care movement – and an increased awareness of the importance of mental health – has been the cornerstone of that change.

The phenomenon had been building for some time, but Ellen at Making Waves points to the pandemic as a key tipping point.

'It's definitely a post-Covid thing – that ramping up,' she says. 'We had to change so quickly, there was that sense of community ... and there was that rise of wellness online.'

Social media has put information about a world of therapies, treatments, activities and exercises at people's finger-tips. It's also made it far easier for people to connect with others interested in a particular practice and find related classes and sessions in their area. That means they are not only able to find something that interests them, but they are also more knowledgeable about the wellness world in general.

That's definitely something that Ellen has found. She specialises in sound therapy, which utilises sound and vibration to help people relax, de-stress and even heal. 'The best way to understand it is that we're all like radios on different frequencies, so I use different sounds to re-tune you to whatever frequency you need to be on,' she says.

Ellen has been exposed to alternative therapies her whole life – her mother is a reiki master – but for a long time she says that marked them out as black sheep within their family. When she started her training as a sound therapist the field was seen as – at best – fringe. She had to work hard to recruit people as case studies because most people had never heard of it and even fewer people were using it. Now, though, she says most people are at least aware of the practice – and open to its potential benefits.

'Now we're at the point where, if I mention sound therapy or mantra, people know what it is,' she says. 'That's a big jump in six or seven years.'

Only skin deep

But while the explosion in wellness is absolutely linked to young people prioritising their health – both physical and mental – it has plenty to do with their physical appearance too. Because, while looking after the way you look is nothing new, this generation has taken it to the next level.

The Hair and Beauty Industry Confederation (HABIC) Ireland said the country spent €2.6 billion on beauty treatments and cosmetics in 2019 (with a further €500 million alleged to be going to operators in the black market – bringing total spend here above €3 billion). That figure includes things like hair, nails and facial appointments, as well as consumer spend on cosmetics and skincare products.

HABIC's data suggested that spend in the sector had risen by more than 26 per cent when compared to 2014 – the starting point for Ireland's post-crash recovery. Under the hood, though, the nature of the spend has seen an even more remarkable shift.

A 2007 report by Mintel suggested that the average Irish woman spent just over €70 a year on cosmetics. A similar survey by online shopping site picodi.com in 2020 pushed that annual spend to €393 – which, even accounting for inflation, is a remarkable ramping up in cosmetic expenditure.

Young adults are major drivers of that shift. While teens and 20-somethings would always have been spenders within the cosmetic industry, they are foregoing the traditional rite of passage of buying the cheap-and-cheerful chemist-shop stuff that will ensure they have plenty of old photos of themselves to cringe at in the future. We're not talking about Pan Stik and Dream Matte Mousse any more – young adults today tend to command a cosmetics arsenal that would make a 1990s beautician blush (and naturally, at that).

PwC's *Voice of the Consumer Sentiment* survey from May 2024 reflects this. It found that 35 per cent of 18–34-year-olds were planning to increase their spending on health and beauty within the next 12 months, compared to 28 per cent of the overall population. Meanwhile the Picodi survey, which looked at spending by consumers in nine countries – including the US, Germany and Italy – placed Irish women as the second-highest cosmetic spenders, beaten only by the Brits. Interestingly, though, it also reflected some of that 'frugal yet flaithiúlach' approach that we can find apparent in young Irish consumer consciousness, as the majority of buyers here said they were mostly motivated by price.

The Picodi survey does have a number of blind spots, though. It is somewhat sexist in its approach – understandably, given the fact that women are by far the biggest spenders in the make-up category. However, in focusing solely on them, it misses out on the niche but rapidly growing business of make-up for men (which often comes wrapped in manly labels like 'War Paint', in order to survive contact with the Masculine Egosystem).

Another blind spot is that it focuses specifically on make-up – ignoring entirely the explosion in spending on skincare products. Interestingly this didn't go unnoticed by the authors of the Mintel report, despite the fact that their survey was conducted way back in 2007. It spotted that the biggest growth area in the Irish cosmetics market was luxury skincare products aimed at the under 30s.

That is now a multibillion-dollar market globally – and while it may have been on the up nearly 20 years ago, it was the pandemic that seems to have brought it to the dizzying heights it's reached today. Irish pharmacies have reported remarkable sales growth in skincare products since 2020, and they say the category grew by 9 per cent last year alone. That's more than any other product category in health and beauty. Those in the industry attribute this recent stellar performance to Covid lockdowns, which gave consumers a chance to step back from their traditional make-up routines.

That time to reconnect with their bare skin was combined with their broader attempts to focus on general wellness. And from that foundation, many people – male and female – have developed elaborate skincare routines, which have only gotten more sophisticated (and probably expensive) over time.

But just as with their physical and mental wellness, tech and social media have also played a critical role. The fact that people are seeing more of their own faces than ever before – on Zoom calls and in Instagram posts – has been a driver. Meanwhile a seemingly limitless number of YouTubers, Instagram Influencers and TikTok talking heads now offer a detailed breakdown of their skincare regime – as well as their make-up processes. They also, rather helpfully, showcase the products they prefer (which they may or may not be getting paid for).

This works, too. A 2023 consumer survey by PwC found that more than half of young Irish adults turned to social media to gather information on a product before they hit the 'buy' button. That compares with 28 per cent of the general population. And while TV ads are still the most common way that older adults are influenced to make a purchase, people in their late teens and 20s are far more inclined to get their heads turned by social-media ads. A whopping 43 per cent of 18–25-year-olds are influenced by these kinds of adverts, it found, compared to the national average of 31 per cent. The survey shows that that influence weighs all the heavier on young shoulders when there's a famous face attached: 38 per cent of young adults said they were motivated to buy by a famous influencer (or 'skinfluencer' as some have dubbed them) or celebrity, compared with 20 per cent of the general population.

And, of course, brands haven't missed out on any of this – they've been quick to hop on board so as not to be left behind by this younger consumer, with all their lovely disposable income. In the space of just a few years, these companies' massive marketing budgets have done an about turn – shifting from focusing on the older woman who is trying to 'fight the signs of ageing' to the 20-something who is trying to pre-empt them altogether.

That's coincided with an explosion in the number of skincare and make-up brands – the most successful of which tend to have a celebrity name attached to them. Rihanna may be a multi-platinum-selling artist capable of selling more than 1.6 million tickets in a single nine-month-long tour, but she became a billion-aire because of her Fenty Beauty cosmetics line.

My personal aesthetic

'It's just the joy of having a really fresh, smooth face – and when that's gone it's just a bit "Oh no",' says Sophie. She's a 34-year-old flight attendant, currently living in her parents' house in Dublin.

Sophie has been getting Botox injections since she was in her late 20s and, with each course of treatment lasting around three months, it's a fairly regular appointment on her calendar. And she's not alone in that, either.

That's because the modern beauty industry – even the part of it that sits on the high street or in your local shopping centre – is about more than just facials and makeovers. There are now also the 'aesthetic' bars and clinics, demand for which has exploded post-pandemic.

These are the businesses that specialise in non-surgical interventions – like Botox injections and dermal fillers – as well as a range of other treatments that promise to tone muscle, dissolve fat, even out skin tone and even reduce sweating. These can often sit side-by-side with more 'traditional' beauty treatments – or be a separate entity altogether. Either way, this is a fast-moving trend in a rapidly emerging sector – and it's a global phenomenon. Money spent on this is on top of all the money being spent on cosmetic procedures and skincare products.

The International Society of Aesthetic Plastic Surgery (ISAPS) estimated that almost 35 million cosmetic procedures were conducted worldwide in 2023. That would represent a 40 per cent increase on the pre-pandemic figure. That figure includes all manner of procedures – from Botox to breast implants, nose jobs to non-surgical fat reduction.

Much like skincare products, these kinds of treatments would previously have been seen as the preserve of an older demographic – the ageing man or woman who opts for a jab or a nip and/or tuck in a last-ditch attempt to cling to their youth. Unlike skincare, these procedures would have been very much the preserve of the better-off. And traditionally there was a fair bit of stigma attached to the scene, too. Getting treatment was a private thing and tabloids and gossip magazines alike were forever on the hunt for any sign that a big name had gotten work done – because doing so was a clear sign of desperation on their part. They should just grow old gracefully, we were told.

But not anymore.

'James and I opened first in 2014 and it was a sideline to our surgical careers,' says Dr Brian Cotter, co-founder of aesthetic chain Sisu. 'The space at the time was not what it is now.'

Brian and James have seen a dramatic change in the decade or so since they set up shop. Cosmetic procedures are no longer kept secret for fear of mockery; nowadays they are a very normal – and in some circles almost expected – part of a young person's routine.

When Brian and James started they were looking for a side hustle that would help them clear their sizeable university debts quicker than their surgeons' incomes would allow. But today the business has grown to 25 locations across Ireland, England and the US, with plans for more to be opened soon. And as part of that dramatic growth in demand for its services has come a significant change in who comes through the doors, too.

'The demographic of our patients has changed,' Brian says. 'You previously had somebody who was in their late 40s, early 50s, probably the ageing factors had caught up with them – and they were coming into the clinic looking for solutions to problems, I guess.

'But it went from that demographic into early 40s, then late 30s, then mid-30s, then early 30s and then into the 20s.'

Sophie – and her cabin crew colleagues – are proof of that. 'Most of the girls I work with – even the guys – they get Botox,' she says.

And she's not at all worried about the potential impact of being a Botox-er from such a young age – she hasn't had any negative side-effects from it, and one of her colleagues has been getting regular treatments for much longer. She's in her 50s but looks like she's 30, apparently. If Sophie does see a downside to being a Botox-er, it's that she likes the results too much.

'The only thing about Botox is it's quite addictive,' she says. 'Once the lines do start coming back, when the Botox wears off, you kind of go "Oh my God!"'

And this trend of more patients seeking more treatments from a younger age is reflected across the industry globally.

According to the ISAPS figures, within the five most common treatments (breast augmentation, liposuction, rhinoplasty, Botox, non-surgical fat reduction) people aged 18 to 34 years old accounted for more than a third of all procedures globally in 2023. A quarter of all Botox treatments worldwide were received by 18–34-year-olds in 2023. They got a combined 2.1 million botulinum toxin injections over the course of that year alone. That age group also had more than 755,000 rhinoplasties that year – making up nearly two-thirds of the total number. They had more than a million breast augmentations – over half of the total number globally.

This is part of a new wave of 'prejuvenation' treatments – though it is also often referred to with names like 'preventative Botox', 'baby Botox' or 'tweakments'. This has seen people in their early 20s seek out procedures before they have any real 'need' for them.

'The space has gone from anti-ageing to wellness, preventative and now we're entering into what we call the prejuvenation space,' says Brian.

The hope among these customers is that by going under the needle early they can stay one step ahead of wrinkles and any other terrible, horrifying, perfectly natural changes that might otherwise happen to their faces. And it's no longer seen as an extreme step – it's almost the norm.

'My mother, who's 72, was into the very expensive anti-wrinkle creams and lotions,' says Brian. 'If you say anti-wrinkle cream to somebody now who's in their mid-to-late 20s, they'll start laughing and say, "Well, actually, that's called Botox."'

The normalisation of getting regular aesthetic treatments coincides with an entire generation of people living out their lives on social media nowadays – and following influencers who are being more honest about what they're doing to their bodies than the models and celebs of old may have been. It also doesn't do any harm that getting a bit of work done today requires little more effort than a short trip down the road.

'I think it's the thing that's in now, it's normal,' says Sophie. 'It's not a big procedure and it's not a secret that people have anymore. It's like getting your hair done.'

And Brian likens this to people who have made the gym a part of their daily or weekly routine. They might be doing this for some short-term goals, but they're also thinking about the advantages it will bring to their longer-term health too. But he also draws a line between the sector's growth and the economic predicament young people find themselves in.

'If they're trying to save for a mortgage or trying to save for something that sometimes is just unobtainable, where the goal-posts keep on moving, I think they want to do something for themselves and they want to do something relatively immediate that will give them a sense of betterment,' he says.

Sophie and her partner are currently saving for a mortgage, too, and hope to be in a position to buy in the not-too-distant future. And while she's spending €300 on Botox every three months, at no point has she felt like it's getting in the way of her need to save. For her, it's about setting aside €25 a week for herself.

'I don't smoke, I don't really drink, I don't go out much. The last time we went out was maybe a month ago and it was a couple of drinks and a burger,' she says. She likes to catch up with friends, but oftentimes, that's done by going for a walk in the park or having a chat over coffee.

'So, I'm not really spending my money on other things,' she says. 'We're all allowed to treat ourselves and this is the way I treat myself.'

Safety and snake oil

Some have pointed to the rise of the Kardashians – and their carefully crafted looks – as the moment when public attitudes towards cosmetic surgery shifted. Really, though, there's no watershed moment for when cosmetic procedures went from being the slightly shameful secret of older people to being the aspirational ideal for the young.

But the fact that we all have a high-powered camera with a 4K screen permanently in our pockets has to be at least a significant factor. We see a lot more of ourselves now than we used to – and we show our faces off a lot more often, too. It's one thing to live with a wrinkle you spot in the mirror from time to time; it's another thing to live with one that's permanently posted for all the world to pinch-zoom in on. And the more we look at ourselves, the more acceptable cosmetic surgery seems to become. Internet search data and anecdotal evidence from cosmetic surgeons shows there was a spike in interest in procedures after the initial wave of pandemic lockdowns, which was attributed to people spending so much of their days on video group chats. It was dubbed within the industry as the Zoom Boom.

'It introduced a patient demographic who openly in a million years, would not have had an aesthetic treatment before,' says Brian. 'What's interesting is friends of mine who are males, who were never in the space, they were on video calls for such long periods of hours that what they started to notice is certain asymmetries in their face or certain things that hadn't bothered them but did annoy them now.'

He says under-eye treatments became particularly popular in the wake of the pandemic, as an increasing number of people felt that they were looking tired. And the flip side of that everyday access to technology seems to have been a driving factor in all of this, because it also made people more aware of just how common aesthetic and cosmetic procedures were becoming; that took away much of the stigma that had existed and fed more demand for services.

'We all have these phones and I think people are now desensitised to it,' he says. 'Previously these treatments would have been – I wouldn't say behind closed doors, but they were very private, and now, when you go onto Instagram or TikTok, it's very mainstream.'

And the fact that people have greater access to treatments, and less shame about wanting to 'improve' their looks, isn't exactly a bad thing. But younger people becoming significant consumers of the aesthetic and cosmetic industries does create new problems. At the very least, adjusting your image with the likes of Botox or dermal fillers at a young age means you are potentially locking yourself into a regular expense for the long term. A common response to a new tattoo is 'Do you not worry how it will look when you're older?' – but, however it looks, at least the tattoo wouldn't have been charging you rent every six months for the past 30 years. And what might start out as a few 'tweakments' can be a slippery slope to a more radical image adjustment if the patient is not careful and discerning.

'We call it "filler blindness", and basically that is both a perception and perspective of the person who is carrying out the treatments,' says Brian. 'I always say to people, if you walk into a practice and your injector provider looks like maybe you don't want to look, you need to leave – because what happens is that their view of what aesthetically looks good, they're going to place that onto you.' (Although it should also be said that there are some who are intentionally seeking out this heavily filled and Botox-ed look.)

On top of all this, customers need to be discerning about where they direct their money for other reasons, because the wellness space in general is almost custom-made for trickery. A quest for self-improvement is a noble way to find more meaning in your life – but maybe the desire to succeed in this realm serves to make people more susceptible to scurrilous scammers.

It's not like we humans need to be encouraged to find a way to rip each other off. The term 'snake oil salesman' goes back to the eighteenth century, referencing the kind of travelling huckster who would promise all sorts of cures and treatments. Panacea was originally the name of a Greek goddess of the universal remedy. The elixir of life was first referenced in a poem from 2100 BC.

But the modern world has made wellness scams even easier money. Here you have a rapidly developing space with lots of medical and scientific terminology, all being avidly consumed by a very online audience keen to better themselves (and willing to spend in order to do so). That has led to no shortage of iffy 'wellness' products and services – not to mention less-than-honest influencers. Remarkably the least-worst offenders here are probably the ones who just lure the audience into parting with their cash in return for little more than a placebo. Others, though, are actively putting customers in harm's way – be it the black-market sellers of Botox-like injections, as uncovered by *RTÉ Investigates*, or those who sell treatments that only serve to harm those looking for help.

Brian Cotter says that while the demand has exploded and the money involved in the industry is now significant, there remains a significant lack of legislation and regulation of operators. That, he says, leaves the door open for cowboy operators.

Though there are dodgy practices in all areas of wellness, not just from those who sell their goods and services on the high street, there has also been a disturbing number of online wellness influencers who have convinced audiences that they have cured life-threatening diseases or serious ailments through some alternative diet or supplement – including Belle Gibson, who is now the subject of a Netflix crime drama. Even a step below straight-up scammers is the growing concern that wellness may be detrimental when directed at the wrong audience. One example of this is how those intensive and intricate skincare regimes can pose a risk – but are attractive nonetheless – to children and teens alike.

And some believe that even the concept of wellness can be a risk factor to some – regardless of what kinds of products or practices you're talking about – because there is an argument that, however well-intentioned it may be, the all-encompassing nature of the movement can ultimately pose a risk to the health of young adults.

'The benefits, of course, like longevity, fewer heart attacks and strokes – all of that we know,' says chartered counselling psychologist Niamh Delmar. 'But wellness is multifaceted and a lot of the social-media wellness that's marketed is from people who don't necessarily have qualifications.

'They're not experts – they might be an influencer, and they're not always evidence-based. So, there can be a lot of unhelpful advice out there.'

This might mean a person wastes a lot of time or money pursuing a line of wellness that doesn't actually work as promised. But as frustrating as this is in its own right, it could also take a mental toll on them – especially if the person blames themselves for the 'failure' rather than realising that the product or service they were sold was the problem. And if they're putting too much of a focus on wellness – and putting too much weight into what benefits it will bring them – they could end up losing sight of the fact that it's supposed to be a means to an end. The result is that their focus on wellness might have the opposite effect to what's intended.

'The standards are too high to reach, and then there can be negative judgements of those that aren't up to standard,' says Niamh.

Oftentimes, too, those negative judgements aren't coming from others – but from ourselves. Because even a media-literate viewer can easily fall into the trap of the social-media stars who paint the picture of a perfect life. And it can be easy to forget that the perfection they're showing is undoubtedly quite different to their unedited reality; or the fact that the wonderful lifestyle they're showing is funded by the viewers of their social-media channel who have bought into their claims. And they often may make it seem as though their idyllic existence can be yours if you follow their lead (and, almost certainly, buy their product or subscribe to their service while you're at it).

The truth is that, while wellness influencers might imply otherwise, there is no quick fix for happiness. Getting into great physical shape and putting a lot of time and effort (and maybe money) into your looks and mindfulness has the potential to be a very good thing – it might even be a great thing. But it's also not going to be as easy as some make it seem, nor is it going to be the solution to all of your ills. And the problem arises when the reality of the pursuit and the frustration of the inevitable failures along the way start to take their toll. 'My social-media idol didn't post about struggling like this – so there must be something wrong with me' is the mental pitfall that many may find themselves in. Even if they eventually reach whatever goal it is they're pursuing, it doesn't automatically make them happy; they might easily turn that on themselves too.

Ultimately, by using wellness as a route to happiness, there's a chance that young people are actually making themselves miserable in the process.

'There's kind of a myth that if you do this, you'll be happy. But that's not true,' says Niamh. 'We know from the World Health Organization that young people's happiness report isn't good in general.

'So even though they have this trend towards wellness and the obsession, sometimes, towards wellness, it's not resonating for a lot of people – because their reports of feeling happy and psychologically well doesn't match it.'

It's Not Easy Being Green

I'm working on a theory that the Irish state once sent every home in Ireland a Richard Clayderman record. Maybe it was some state-sponsored stimulus scheme for the music industry. Perhaps we did some kind of cultural exchange with France that saw us ship over millions of Chieftains records in return for all these easy listening piano pressings. Or maybe it was in the hope that his new romantic style would help further stimulate the country's birth rate.

I should say, I haven't found much hard evidence for this theory – yet. All I'm working with so far is the impossible-to-ignore fact that, if you go to almost any charity shop in the country and flick through the stack of vinyls they have, it won't take you long before you'll see Richard Clayderman's face staring back at you. And I reckon there has to be a deeper reason for this. It can't be that so many Irish people willingly bought his records.

I find further circumstantial evidence for my theory at Oxfam's shop in Ringsend, Dublin. It has a fairly small vinyl section – positioned just after you walk in the front door – and Clayderman's is one of the records on offer. But I'm not here to see what dirt-cheap, obscure vinyl this charity shop has on offer. Not this time, anyway. I'm here to find out about clothes.

Oxfam has 45 shops on the island of Ireland but its Ringsend branch is one of its busiest for clothing donations. That's in part because of its central location – with some donors travelling cross-country to get here – and in part because it has a reputation for trying to make the most of what people hand in. I can see that in action in the sorting room at the back of the shop. Standing here, I'm surrounded by racks and racks of tops, dresses, jumpers and shirts. There are shelves full of ornaments and household items, kids' books and board games. And floorspace is at a premium, with bags and bags of unsorted items at our feet. According to Oxfam Ireland's donated goods strategy manager Mark Sweeney, this is what an average day here looks like.

He explains that some charity shops might take a fairly straight-forward approach to pricing donations – for example, pricing a jumper at €5 and a dress at €10, no matter what it might have been worth if sold new. That approach can make it easier for a charity shop to process donations and probably makes the odd eagle-eyed bargain hunter very happy. But it does mean the shop risks missing out on potential revenue and, according to Mark, it can put off some of the more discerning donors, because the Ringsend shop often gets donations of high-end items that have been well looked after – or not worn at all. In the sorting room, I spot one designer dress with the tag still on it. And while the people handing these items in may have no more use for them, they know they're worth something – and they don't like the idea of the charity getting anything less that the most out of the dona-tion they've made.

I suppose for us normals, it would be akin to spending the month siphoning all of your spare change into the Trócaire box only to find out that they throw away anything smaller than a €1 coin.

But taking a more considered approach, as Oxfam does, takes time and skill. Donated items have to be carefully checked – not just to see if they can be sold at all but to see exactly what con-dition are they in. Are they brand new and unworn? Maybe only worn once? Fairly worn in but not worn out? Then it's a case of figuring out what they're worth new – or what a similar item might sell for. Knowing what kinds of things sell well – and for how much – helps too. What season we're in and what the weather is doing can matter too, and having an awareness of what is on-trend at the moment, and what might be considered timeless, is also important. But there's no formula for this – there's no price list the volunteers can refer to when deciding how to price each item and no guide they can pass on to new recruits. It's essentially an instinct that people hone over time, until they're able to get a gut feeling about an item within seconds of picking it up.

And all of this is done in the back of the Ringsend shop – with some of the stock then going out on the shop floor. Some of it is also sent on to other Oxfam branches – especially ones that might not get as many donations – and, over time, stock that doesn't sell is rotated around the branches in the hope that it will eventually find its buyer.

It's a lot of work but it gets results. As proof of that, Mark says the shop's social media is closely watched by fashionistas. When it occasionally posts about a high-end item it's received – like a luxury handbag – there's usually someone in the shop within the hour looking to buy it. It's not a price point that tempts them, either. In fact, the shop doesn't publicise prices when promoting items online. Those watching know they'll be paying more than bargain basement prices – but they see it as good value all the same.

It's a well-oiled machine that seems to work well for everyone involved – the donor, the charity and the shopper. But there's a problem. Because, in recent years, the machine has started to become clogged.

Fast as you scan

Mark reckons the pandemic was a turning point.

'Before Covid, it would have been very much your normal people – we have our charity shop customers, they would have been of a certain demographic, they would have been a bit older,' he says. 'There was a bit of consciousness about what people were buying, but it wasn't as purpose-driven as it is now.'

The retail landscape has shifted dramatically since the pre-pandemic days, too, he says.

'Brands like Shein and Temu didn't really exist pre-Covid, so it was a different world. There was still fast fashion and there was still hyper-consumerism – but it wasn't to the level that happened after Covid.'

And he ties all of this in with the rise of online shopping – one of the big beneficiaries of the lockdowns and an approach that he believes makes hyper-consumption easier. At the same time, though, he says lockdowns seem to have led to more consumers becoming eco-conscious and aware of what these kinds of shopping habits are doing to the planet.

'We've seen a massive increase in that younger generation shopping with us – where maybe pre-Covid it was a smaller cohort of them, but it's definitely increased.'

And that's all translated into a rise in the quantity of products they receive as donations. Since the pandemic, he says that the volume of donations they're receiving has increased dramatically. But the amount of high-end goods they're taking in has remained largely static – the increase has been almost entirely confined to the low-end of the clothing spectrum: the cheap, fast-fashion fodder that so many retail empires are now built upon.

This presents a problem for a charity like Oxfam. These cheap items are often poor quality and not really suitable for resale – but time still needs to be devoted to identifying and sorting through them. And, even when items are in good enough condition to be sold, it can be hard to justify doing so.

'When you buy something online for three or four quid – OK, great value – but then you decide "Ah I've only spent three quid on it, it doesn't matter, I can throw it into the charity shop"; then, when the charity shop gets it, even if it has its tags on it, even if it's brand new, we can't sell it for three quid. So, then we have to sell it for, maybe, a euro.

'And then who's going to buy it for one euro when they could buy it for three online? Plus, people come into charity shops and they don't want to be presented with ultra-fast fashions … so it becomes a challenge of how we sell the product.'

That means a lot of time and effort goes into getting these items processed, priced and on display – and the charity will, at best, make a tiny return on them. But perhaps more realistically, clothing may simply end up getting disposed of at the end of this labour-intensive process (though Mark assures me that Oxfam tries to do this disposal in as sustainable a way as possible too).

But there's a conundrum here for Oxfam, too, because while these kinds of donations are of little or no value to them – and potentially even costly – they don't want to discourage them, either. Doing so, they fear, could put people off donating altogether. Instead, they'd rather deal with the crap in the hope that it creates a habit among consumers. Maybe they'll become charity shop buyers in the process. Maybe they'll eventually become more ethical in their shopping habits. What's important is they're not sent off feeling like they got scolded for trying to do the right thing.

'We're trying to get them to consider what they're buying in the first place,' he says. 'There's an analogy – you can put as many holes in a sink as you want but if you don't turn off the tap in the first place, it's going to overflow.'

And that's the problem from the consumer point of view, too.

Fast fashion has normalised the idea of disposable clothing – with cheap, often poorly made items being shipped across the world to be worn once. In the past, people might have tried to avoid wearing the same outfit to two separate family events, for fear that someone would notice. Now, they try to avoid wearing the same outfit in two Instagram posts. No-one really needs to be told that fast fashion is bad for the environment – nor do they need to be reminded of the ethical issues many supply chains have. But the market for these kinds of products remains huge nonetheless.

Part of the reason for that relates back to the surge in low-end donations places like Oxfam are seeing. Fast-fashion buyers are donating their pre-loved but now unwanted items – and probably feeling good about themselves for doing so. Maybe they feel like they're cancelling out the negatives of their original purchase. And, sure enough, donating rather than dumping the item is a kind of positive – but nowhere near enough to counter the damage that was done at the original point of purchase.

Fast-fashion donors have found themselves facing the Clayderman Contradiction. Just like the original owners of those records, they got their hands on something – maybe after a rush of blood to the head – only to realise all too soon that they don't want or need it after all. Faced with a choice of either dumping it altogether or donating it, they choose the latter – convincing themselves that it's the more responsible and ethical decision. But it was a false choice in the first place. Because now the charity shop has to deal with an item that no-one else wants – even at a low, low price. In the end, after the charity shop has put a lot of effort into selling or reusing or recycling any unwanted item before it ends up going to landfill or incineration, there's a good chance it will end up getting dumped after all.

If people thought about it they'd probably realise the contradiction that was at the heart of their good deed – but as long as it's someone else doing the dumping, they can take themselves off the hook for their problematic spending.

Put on the green jersey

All of this represents an interesting contradiction within the Bailout Babies, because they are arguably the most environmentally and ethically clued-in generation of all time. They would put the ultimately niche Flower Power movement of the 1960s to shame in terms of how broad and mainstream their progressive attitudes are.

A 2022 survey by the Young Social Innovators found that climate change was a major concern for 78 per cent of young adults – with 87 per cent saying the government was not doing enough to tackle the problem. A CSO study found that people aged 18 to 34 were far more concerned about climate change than any other age group – and had above-average levels of concern about air pollution and the potential loss of biodiversity too. And they were ready to let these views inform some major life decisions. A survey by the Economic and Social Research Institute (ESRI) found that young people wanted more radical action taken on climate change – and were willing to change the way they lived their lives for the cause. That included flying less and reducing the amount of meat they consumed. Meanwhile, a 2023 survey by the European Investment Bank found that 70 per cent of 20–29-year-olds take the climate impact of a company into consideration when job hunting, with 17 per cent seeing it as a top priority.

There's probably a degree of selfishness in that – and that's perfectly understandable. After all, younger people are the ones who are more likely to face the negative consequences of climate change and rampant pollution, and they know waiting for change is only going to make things worse. It's perfectly reasonable for them to demand something is done now, so that they might not have to face the worst of what will come if everything stays the same. They're also better informed about the issues and the impact humans are having on the planet – and they're far more outward looking than previous generations, not just in terms of environmentalism, either. Young adults here are more socially and ethically aware, too. A 2019 Eurobarometer survey found that 87 per cent of 15–30-year-olds were active participants in social, political and civic activities. So, these things matter to them, and they want them to matter to companies too, with a Youth Lab survey by Thinkhouse finding that 29 per cent of young adults expect brands to be ethical and responsible and conduct their business fairly and sustainably. And a 2021 survey by Youth Work Ireland found that 82 per cent of young people wanted to avoid fast fashion altogether – not just because of the environmental impact but also because of the often ethically weak practices that feature in its supply chains.

And, yet, they can't seem to manage to follow through on their good intentions.

A 2021 report by the Environmental Protection Agency estimated that women aged 16 to 34 made up the highest proportion of females who were 'high frequency purchasers' – they were people who tended to buy clothes on a weekly basis and purchase clothes four times as often as a 'low frequency' purchaser. Males were far less inclined to qualify as 'high frequency purchasers', but when they did, it was once again the younger cohort that was over-represented. Young women were more inclined than others to buy an item that they only wore a few times or not at all. They were also more willing to buy fashionable items that they knew they wouldn't keep for long. And the price, style and brand were all more likely to motivate a young adult to purchase – rather than the product's sustainability or environmental impact.

Maybe some of this can be explained away by the same mindset that has created the Little Treat culture – they see these small fast-fashion purchases as a deserved gift to themselves. They know the damage their purchasing is doing and they want to do something about it. But, for whatever reason, they just can't bring themselves to.

Get that green

So, the Bailout Babies are hypocrites.

The truth is, when it comes to the environment at least, we all are. That being said, committing to buying fewer flimsy tops – made in questionable conditions – seems like a fairly easy win in the grand scheme of going green. But, without wanting to pass the buck completely, their bad eco-habits are being aided and abetted by brands and businesses. The only true form of green consumerism is to buy what you need, when you need it and no more. But that practice doesn't work too well for the companies that are continually seeking sales growth. They are consumption-fuelled machines, and they need to find a way to keep the flow of new spending coming. So, they spend big to get us to spend big.

And the fact that this generation is much more eco-aware than its elders hasn't been missed by big brands, either. If anything, they're painfully aware of that fact as evidenced by consumer surveys and reports in Ireland – and around the world – which continually show that sustainability is not only important to younger people, but it's also a major factor in their spending decisions. Younger consumers say they are more inclined to choose products that are made sustainably, and they say they avoid brands that they know have a poor environmental record. Not only that, these consumers also say they're willing to pay more for 'green' brands. But making a brand sustainable takes time. It's expensive, too. And, as I already mentioned, true sustainability is about encouraging people to buy less – not more. That's all bad for the balance sheet. And so, while some companies have made real headway in going green, others have, instead, invested more of their time and energy into convincing consumers that they have solid eco-credentials – even when that may not be entirely true.

This is a trend that extends beyond clothing – with brands of all type and stripe promising consumers that they are using less, sourcing better and recycling more. This can take the form of sometimes confusing and constantly shifting equations which require a maths qualification to decipher – '20 per cent smaller package made up of 15 per cent recycled material, fully recyclable'. It often involves lots of symbols, as well as some kind of certification scheme which claims to set standards that the companies are striving to hit.

This effort has also seen multiple brands launching recycling initiatives – offering consumers the chance to 'close the loop' by returning their used or old items to their point of origin. Meanwhile others have put a lot of emphasis on the launch of 'sustainable' product lines that claim to be less energy- and resource-intensive while also paying producers fairly for their efforts.

But how much of this represents real change, and how much of it is eco-theatre?

The reality is that, by offering consumers an opportunity to recycle in-store, retailers are, above all else, creating a system that allows us – and them – to wipe away our environmental sins without necessarily doing anything. It's the Clayderman Contradiction all over again – allowing us to feel like we are doing the right thing by properly disposing of old clothes in in-store recycle bins without us having to bother ourselves as to what happens beyond that. And the truth is that not many people can say for sure what does happen to these 'recycled' items. Many in the textile industry question whether the retailers are actually diverting any of those donated products to recycling or reuse – or whether they just end up being shipped to poorer countries and, ultimately, to landfill anyway.

A 2023 investigation by two Swedish journalists showed that this was the end result in the case of at least one major fast-fashion retailer. They put 10 items into H&M recycling boxes, each of which had a Bluetooth tracker hidden inside. Five months later, none of the items had ended up going to the sorting centres of the retailer's recycling partners, while some were ultimately sent thousands of kilometres away to landfills in places like Ghana.

Even when items do go to be recycled, the end result is only slightly better. It's estimated that just 1 per cent of recycled clothes are turned back into new garments – in part due to the cost involved in re-manufacturing existing materials. This is why big retailers' 'sustainable' and 'recycled' product lines are so rare and often based around a small range of clothes. They are, at best, a token gesture. A further 10–15 per cent of recycled textiles might get 'down-cycled' – which means reused as rags, mop-heads or mattress filling. Most of what's left ultimately gets dumped. But brands' recycling schemes aren't just there to make us feel better – or to make us feel like the brand is trying. They are also an opportunity for companies to shield themselves from criticism. We've made it possible to recycle, they say, so the ball is in the consumer's court.

A good example of that is Nestlé's Nespresso coffee pods – which have become hugely popular in the past decade. They've replaced Maxwell House as the default coffee option in your average home – which even the snobbiest of coffee snobs has to be grateful for. But at the same time, the rise of these machines has created tonnes of waste; waste that didn't exist when other forms of coffee-making were being relied upon. That, understandably, prompted significant criticism of Nestlé which, in response, created a Nespresso pod recycling programme. This scheme allows customers to return their used pods to Nestlé – for free – with the Swiss company then doing the hard work of taking them apart, cleaning them out and recycling their component parts. Which all sounds very good.

But the most recent data published by the company shows that only a third of its pods are returned and recycled. That means somewhere in the region of 10 billion pods are being dumped each year (and that figure is just for the official Nespresso-brand pods – it doesn't include the billions of pods made by other brands like Douwe Egberts, Bewley's, Costa etc.). But hey, that's not Nestlé's fault; that's down to the lazy consumer. The scheme effectively allows Nestlé to side-step the problem its product is creating and point the finger back at us.

Big companies have been muddying the polluted waters in other ways, too. Big brands like Nestlé, Cadbury's and Coca-Cola like to make big announcements about their environmental targets – but there is little or no real oversight to keep them in check. When Coca-Cola this year extended the deadline for its own recycling targets, while simultaneously reducing the target itself, no-one swooped in to issue a fine or demand compensation. Organisations like Fair Trade and Rainforest Alliance may once have been seen as the kind of independent (but ultimately powerless) arbiter of a brand's sustainability, but even here, many have abandoned these standards in favour of their own. Cadbury's, for example, ditched Fair Trade in 2019, in favour of its parent company's own 'Cocoa Life' scheme. Nestlé followed suit a year later, with its own 'Cocoa Plan' programme taking the place of the green, black and blue logo.

Meanwhile, the last refuge of the greenwashing scoundrel comes in the form of now widely questioned carbon-offsetting schemes – where companies can pay to have their emissions compensated for elsewhere. The concept here is that a polluter 'buys' the emissions that have been avoided through green energy schemes, or they invest in the planting of enough trees to theoretically capture the emissions they are producing. Except the accountability in these schemes is often lacklustre at best, and there have been countless examples of double-selling emissions savings – meaning multiple companies are taking credit for the same thing. Meanwhile, while planting lots of trees may make for a nice photo op, the reality is that it takes years for those to do anything in terms of capturing carbon – and that only happens if the saplings are protected and maintained, which often isn't the case. Often what these carbon offsetters are doing is finding a very roundabout way to pay for bird feed.

But none of that really matters because the actual environmental benefits of these programmes are generally, at best, secondary.

The primary aim of investing in recycling programmes, sustainability standards and carbon offsetting schemes is to convince the consumer that the brand is doing right by the planet. It is a way of reassuring us that our hyper-consumption is okay. It glosses over the fact that no amount of green schemes and recycling initiatives can counter the environmental impact of a product that never had a reason to exist in the first place. And, to be honest, they're often pushing an open door on this. Because we may want to be more environmentally friendly – but we also want to buy that new thing, too.

Rise and Shein

It is also worth bearing in mind the context of our consumer habits, though. It's not just that our sustainability concerns are being placated – we are also continually under assault from the carefully crafted consumption machine.

Companies wanting us to give them more of our money is nothing new – nor is the cynical messaging that tells us This One Product™ is the solution to all our fears, doubts and body issues. The difference today is that people are bombarded with a near-relentless stream of targeted ads and encouragement trying to get them to part with their cash. The more tech-engaged the consumer is, and the more disposable income they have to spend, the more focused on them that machine becomes – and the better job it can do of exploiting their vulnerabilities.

In other words, the Bailout Babies are the perfect victims.

Fast-fashion retailers have long since evolved beyond the idea of having 'seasons' in favour of 'collections', with new lines of products constantly hitting the virtual shelves. Consequently, there's a constant churn now, with major retailers using what's called the 'test and repeat' model, where small batches of new products are constantly being ordered. Any lines that sell well are re-ordered and the ones that perform poorly are dumped. It's estimated that just 6 per cent of Shein's inventory remains in stock for more than 90 days. Globally, upwards of 100 billion items of clothing are produced each year – this is the equivalent of each person on the planet getting a new item each and every month of the year. But, of course, no-one needs that kind of rolling stock of new pieces of clothing – and so that constant churn of products is built on the idea that there is always a buyer who can be convinced that they need something new. People need to be given serious encouragement to consume at a rate that justifies that level of manufacturing.

To make that happen, retailers have teams of designers, buyers and market-watchers whose entire function is to spot the latest micro-trend that they can capitalise on, turning around dupes and zeitgeist-friendly fashions in no time at all. They recruit celebrities of all status to help lend these efforts some heft – from big name singers, actors and models all the way to whichever sculpted socialite happened to catch their eye in the latest season of *Love Island*. And once they've hopped on a trend and slapped their minor celebrity's name on the label, they blanket-bomb would-be and have-been customers with promotional emails, push notifications, discount codes and 'last chance to buy' warnings. (This kind of rapid-fire buzz-seeking machine is also why there have been so many cases of big retailers stealing the designs of small artists too, as mentioned in an earlier chapter.)

Haul of famer

Twenty-three-year-old Rachel rents a tiny room in north Dublin, paying mortgage prices for the privilege of sharing a bathroom with four total strangers. She's done her best to make the space her own – decking it out in floral prints, pink fairy lights, retro wall art and kitschy cushions shaped like fish – despite not having much money to spare for the likes of interior decorating. Because Rachel is a Shein Queen; someone who's mastered the art of the deal – at least when it comes to bagging Chinese clutter on the cheap. She has figured out what it takes to maximise discounts, she can hunt down coupon codes in seconds, and she never, ever pays for shipping. She's so good at it, she's even amassed an enviable following on Instagram, where she showcases her latest finds.

Our Shein Queen isn't a mere shopper anymore; she's a player. In a world that constantly reminds her of what she doesn't have, this is one place where she can feel like a winner. Only the shops that she's buying from don't feel like they're on the losing end of the deal. In fact, Rachel is close to their ideal customer – someone who's convinced they're getting a bargain, and spends more as a result. Because many big digital retailers have mastered the art of gamifying retail – with visitors to sites like Temu regularly being prompted to avail of discount codes (which become more generous the more you spend), roulette wheel 'freebies' (as long as you spend X amount on other goods) and time-limited offers (that happen to be ending within minutes of you opening the app). It's like what would happen if Penneys and the seaside amusements had a baby.

And this suits our Shein Queen, who might not have much money to spare but feels she can get plenty of bang for her buck on sites like these (if she's willing to ignore the fact that it's mostly cheap tat). While it's getting harder and harder to bag a bargain in the real world, the layers of supposed discounts can at least let her think she's saved a fortune. And while she can't afford major purchases, the buzz she gets hearing a minor one hit her doorstep can fill the dopamine void for a moment ... at least until she opens it up and realises what she bought is already falling apart. The rise of the 'mystery box' has built on this – acting like a lucky dip bag, except for clothing and accessories. So, not only are people being encouraged to spend their money on products they don't really need, they're now spending it on things they haven't even seen.

But trying to squeeze more spending out of previous customers, or those already browsing your app, isn't enough. There needs to be a constant production line of new consumers to feed off. And companies' efforts to find these buyers have been supported by the technologies that have become so central to young people's lives too – because, while social-media companies would like you to focus on the 'social' bit, the reality is that they are just 'media' companies – specifically, ad media companies. For example, Meta – which owns Instagram, Facebook, Threads and WhatsApp – got nearly 98 per cent of its billions in revenue from advertising last year. Alphabet – which owns YouTube and Google – takes about 75 per cent of its earnings from ads too. And while China's ByteDance – owner of TikTok – doesn't disclose its financial information, its balance sheet is also certain to be heavily weighted towards ad revenue.

These firms make hundreds of billions of dollars each year from ads – and they do that by gleaning as much information as possible as they can from users. That means the accounts you follow, the things you post about and the things you watch in-app help to paint a picture about the kind of consumer you are. If you're not extremely careful about your privacy settings they might even be tracking the other sites you're visiting, not to mention the places you visit in real life. And they're doing all of this with your friends too – because if they know they like This One Product™, there's a good chance you'll like it too.

From all of that, they can build a pretty good picture about the kind of person you are – what you do, where you go, what you like and what you aspire to. And with all of that information, the social-media platforms can help companies to construct a perfectly targeted ad – perhaps one that taps into a desire, goal or anxiety. It's good old-fashioned retail therapy – except, in this case, the shop has access to your session notes.

As a result, social-media platforms have become the perfect conduit for fast-fashion brands desperate to create the demand that justifies their supply. Now they can inject the perfect message exactly where the customer's eyes are fixed – just between a heart-warming puppy rescue clip and a compilation of people falling over. But, of course, retailers capitalise on social media in other ways too – taking a more direct approach to getting your cash.

Fast-fashion brands do this by constantly being on the hunt for influencers and Insta-celebs who they can 'partner' with – giving them early and/or free access to new products in return for them advertising the goods on their stream. And the real mark of success for a fast-fashion marketer is when people (like our Shein Queen) do this for free – showing their latest 'Temu Haul' or 'Shein Try On' to their followers of their own accord. Often-times, these are made up of products bought on a whim, with no particular purpose in mind. Sometimes they were bought with the express purpose of them being featured on a video like this. Sometimes they are even bought with the intention of actually being worn at some stage. But whatever the catalyst, the videos show the buyer appraising them for the first time – live. It's almost like they've invited the world into the shop's fitting room – except they're doing so after they've already parted with their cash.

And this has created a dangerous influencer/retailer feedback loop. The retailer loves these 'haul' videos because they essentially represent someone paying to advertise their products. Wannabe influencers also love these videos because they draw eyeballs to their account, which can open the door to them getting money and freebies down the line. Regular punters love them too because they help them see what the products listed on a website look like in real life. Maybe there's a bit of a vicarious shopping buzz thrown in there, too.

But while this may feel to many to be a win-win-win kind of consumption, none of those involved are really feeling the environmental cost of all these items being made, shipped across the world and – quite probably – dumped shortly after. After all, the Shein Queen's box room can only hold so much ornamental clutter and poorly made clobber.

The Clean Clothes Campaign – which aims to improve the ethical and environmental standards in the industry – estimates that as much as 65 per cent of garments end up in landfill within 12 months of being produced.

Of course, some will say that, where they are guilty of over-consumption, they counter that somewhat by returning the products they don't plan on wearing. But it's questionable how much better this is than simply throwing them straight in the bin. Because, not only are online retailers now doing their utmost to discourage returns by adding charges, many also dump the items they do take back. That's because it usually works out as the cheaper option compared to spending time on processing, checking and restocking the items in question. Given that their product lines are going through a continual change, there's a good chance that the item will be behind their trend line by the time it gets returned anyway.

This is all to say that while consumers – and especially young consumers – may have every intention of being more ethical in their habits, they are facing down an entire multi-trillion-dollar industry that seems primed to encourage consumption and generate unnecessary waste from top to bottom. And it's an industry that doesn't mind playing dirty in order to clean up. Without wanting to excuse the hypocrisy of young adults, if global organisations like Oxfam are struggling under the tide of hyper-consumption, the individual consumer is bound to feel helpless too.

But, of course, they're not completely helpless – and one reason for hope is the fact that a growing number of younger adults seem increasingly to be trying to sidestep that hungry industry altogether, through person-to-person resale platforms like Vinted and Depop. These allow people to sell on their unwanted clothes directly – rather than donating or dumping them altogether. And while they may not be perfect – Mark from Oxfam says they are arguably still feeding the consumption machine – they're a significant sight better than the Buy It Today, Bin It Tomorrow model.

'I don't think people buy on Vinted like they buy on Shein, because it's a more considered purchase – they think about the quality. It's funny – people actually think more about quality when they buy second-hand than they do when they buy new.'

Mind the Gap

'No-one knows how to deal with this new phase that we're going through – the rules have changed, the goalposts have moved, but no-one really has a conversation about it.'

Fiona, a former researcher with RTÉ, now counsels parents through a number of organisations – including the Parentline helpline. Through that work she is seeing the first-hand effects that the housing crisis is having on familial relationships and people's mental health.

'It's like the natural evolution has jarred a little bit. There's this kind of stunted development of sorts – the young adult is living at home, but the dynamic has gone from two adults looking after their children to all adults living under the same roof.

'Everything has changed, but nothing has changed.'

The Bailout Babies may be looking ahead to a rapidly deteriorating planet, but what state is the housing crisis leaving their heads in?

Where's your head at?

Well, to take a step back for a second, we know that young adults are struggling more and more with their mental health in general. The *My World Survey 2* from 2019 found that young adults were reporting significantly higher levels of depression than the young adults surveyed in 2012. This increase was across the spectrum, too, with a rise in those reporting mild, moderate, severe and very severe cases. It was a similar story for anxiety, with a notable up-tick in young adults reporting issues in this regard. The percentages reporting moderate, severe or very severe cases all rose considerably between the seven years, with only mild cases remaining static.

In fact, for both depression and anxiety, those having some level of issue went from the minority to the majority in the time span between the two surveys. In 2012, 60 per cent of young adults were categorised as having 'normal' levels of depression. By 2019, it was 45 per cent. For cases of anxiety, those with a 'normal' level fell from 62 per cent in 2012 to 45 per cent in 2019.

And that coincides with a general deterioration in the mood of the country's young adults, because the *My World Survey 2* discovered that young adults also had lower levels of self-esteem and were less optimistic than their equivalents seven years earlier. And they seemed to be having a harder time dealing with this –they got worse at using support-focused or problem-based coping mechanisms but were more inclined to use avoidance-based measures.

Echoing those findings is a 2023 survey by the Health Service Executive (HSE), which found a rise in the percentages of young men and women reporting negative mental health when compared to a similar survey in 2016. That came as the proportion of 15–34-year-olds who rated their overall health as 'good' or 'very good' also declined.

Social media often gets the blame for this and, sure enough, the *My World Survey 2* shows that young adults who spent the most time online were more inclined to be in the 'severe' or 'very severe' categories for depression. Those who spent more than three hours a day online were also more likely to be in the 'very severe' range for anxiety – with those spending less than two hours a day online tending to be in the 'normal' range. Whether this is cause and effect is nearly impossible to know for sure. Are these young adults more depressed and anxious because they spend too much time online? Or are they spending too much time online as a way of managing or distracting them from their depression and/ or anxiety?

That being said, being plugged into the perpetual anger machines that places like X have become certainly doesn't seem like a good thing for a person's mental health. Having the digital equivalent of a front-row seat to war, death and destruction in Gaza and Ukraine, and hate and toxicity in the US and Europe, would surely darken anyone's mood. But even social media's biggest hater would struggle to prove that it's solely responsible for the decline in young people's mental health. The *My World Survey 2* also highlights links between those with good sleep routines and those with 'normal' levels of depression and anxiety. The survey (and many other reports) also points to lower levels of physical activity as a catalyst.

However, social media's growing importance in our day-to-day lives is very much intertwined with another trend that has contributed to young people's declining mental health – the shrinking of real-world social circles – because the young adults of today are also part of a generation that communicates primarily through texts and direct messages. In the *Growing Up in Ireland* survey based on responses from then 20-year-olds, 98 per cent of males and females cited 'spending time online' as a favoured activity, followed by listening to music and, in third place, hanging out with friends. The 2019 *My World Survey 2* found that 30 per cent of young adults spent three or more hours online each day – with a further 30 per cent spending two to three hours a day online.

Clearly, for many, reels have replaced the real.

Fear and living

But is it fair to pin all of this on young people being locked out of the housing market and stuck in their parents' house? Maybe not entirely. The rise in mental health challenges, particularly among young adults, has many mothers – including social media.

That is exposing them to a daily tsunami of digital negativity and unobtainable perfection, and is at least one part of the multi-part-tag-team that's led them to a more isolated life. But as much blame as Instagram and TikTok should take, undesirable living arrangements – and knowing you can't afford to change that – is going to lend significant support to that digital negativity.

'For most adults, money is a source of stress,' says Dr Denis O'Hora – though he adds that measuring the impact of that stress is easier said than done.

'We know financial pressures can lead to mental health problems, but if you look at the detail, you will see that people under different levels of economic hardship aren't necessarily indicators of whether they have anxiety, depression or negative mental health outcomes,' he says. 'If someone has a large mortgage, do you think that they are necessarily under pressure? No, because most people who have large mortgages have large houses and good jobs.'

He and his students are currently trying to develop a framework for better measuring this – focusing on people's subjective feelings about housing scarcity, as opposed to the objective reality.

'It's not because people are inventing problems – but it's the subjective impression people have of their situation … people can tell you what they are, and those are pretty good predictors of whether there's going to be a problem or not.'

And there is already a pool of survey data that draws a clearer line between a young adult's economic situation and their mood. For example, two out of every five Gen Zers (in this case people born between 1995 and 2009) cited housing as a leading issue affecting their mental health. The Amárach Research study for Young Social Innovators put 'fear or anxiety about the future' as a concern for 59 per cent of respondents.

A 2022 survey by Youth Work Ireland found that more than two out of every five 16–24-year-olds did not believe life in Ireland had become better in the previous five years, while a similar proportion were not hopeful that things would improve in the five years ahead. That means these people are braced for a decade, at least, of stagnation. But improvement even beyond that timeframe seems optimistic in the eyes of many young adults. Rather than it being a short-to-mid-term problem, young adults expect that the cost crunch is here to stay.

In fact, the greatest fear of the vast majority of Gen Zers, according to the aforementioned Young Social Innovators study, was the prospect of facing unaffordable living costs in 20 years' time. That was at the front of the minds of 79 per cent of Gen Zers – even managing to outpace fears around the impact of climate change that was cited by 78 per cent of the respondents. The survey also found that being financially secure had become the greatest sign of a successful life in the eyes of these young people – overtaking 'making a difference in your community/the world' as a primary aspiration.

Grim.

Monetary malaise

Being stuck in economic stasis with only financial decline to look forward to doesn't only lower the aspirations of our young would-be innovators. It also drags on our mood and – ultimately – mental health.

The NYCI's *State of Our Young Nation* report shows that young adults had low levels of wellbeing, with their current housing situation and worries about the future to the fore in their minds. It reported that 4 out of 10 18–29-year-olds had felt relaxed 'rarely' or none of the time in the two weeks leading up to the survey. Meanwhile the rising pessimism detected in the *My World Survey 2* was also reflected here, with the NYCI capturing a decline in young people's optimism about the future. This negative outlook appeared to grow as you moved up the age brackets, with those aged 27 to 29 the least optimistic of all.

Concerns around finances, dissatisfaction with pay and conditions and the rising cost of living were all cited as contributing factors in this deteriorating mood. One in five respondents said they had skipped meals due to rising cost pressures.

That has created a generation that is struggling to keep its head above water financially as well as psychologically. One-third of Gen Zers describe the mood of their generation as 'anxious', closely followed by 'stressed' and 'depressed'. Just a handful say their generation is motivated (7 per cent) or enthusiastic (5 per cent). Traditionally, you'd have to binge watch a few years' worth of *Eastenders* to reach that level of despair.

And that feeling of being stuck, under growing financial pressure with no sign of escape, has fed into a broader dissatisfaction with the entire system, it seems. A 2023 survey by The Youth Lab found that 63 per cent of young people did not trust the state to actively govern in their best interests. That was up from 49 per cent in a similar survey just two years before.

Many young adults also seemed to be experiencing a breakdown in the bond they have with authority figures far closer to home, too – literally. The *My World Survey 2* found that 40 per cent of young adults cited conflict with parents as one of the 'stressful life events' they experienced – second only to the numbers who referenced a bereavement. Those who experienced parental conflict were also more likely to report moderate to very severe levels of anxiety or depression.

Needless to say, living at home for longer is only going to increase these people's exposure to – and impact from – this kind of parental conflict.

And this may go some way to explaining why there was a significant decline in the number of young adults saying that they were enjoying family life. In the 2012 iteration of the *My World Survey*, 66 per cent of young adults said they were enjoying it, compared to 32 per cent in 2019. It's easier to be positive about your circumstances when you have some control over them – or, at the very least, the prospect of control in the not-too-distant future. And that lack of control is a key source of stress for these young adults. The survey found that 42 per cent of them cited 'the future' as one of their top stressors, while finances were a major concern for 41 per cent. Only college ranked higher, at 68 per cent.

Interestingly, young adults had become more inclined to speak about these stresses with their family – at 56 per cent compared to 44 per cent in 2012. At the same time, fewer turned to their friends (36 per cent versus 43 per cent). Exactly why this is the case is hard to know, though it's not unreasonable to suggest that it's a reflection of the narrowing social pool referred to above and a consequence of more young adults spending more time in close quarters with their parents.

And the obvious red flag that raises is a situation where the family itself is the source of stress.

Coping strategies

'You could have a very successful business man or business woman in their own right – they could have a great job, but they're going home and living with their parents,' says Fiona. 'And it's going from that hugely responsible role in the workplace to coming home and readjusting to being the child of their parents, because different rules apply at home.

'Really it's easier to have a mature, healthy relationship with adult children and their parents if they live apart.'

If there is a silver lining in all of this, it's that the young adults of today are far more aware of their mental health – and its importance – than their equivalents in previous generations. A survey conducted for Mental Health Ireland late last year found that 94 percent of 25–34-year-olds were doing at least one thing each week for their mental health. Exercise, hobbies or spending time with friends and family were the most popular activities.

But even this doesn't make them immune to the challenges they face – often the same challenges that are weighing on their mental health in the first place. More than 40 per cent of the same age group cited a lack of money as one of the barriers to them supporting their own mental health, with a similar proportion saying they did not have enough time.

So, you're left with a cohort that is increasingly worried about their finances and future, which is making them more depressed and anxious. Many of them may recognise this and are trying to do something to mitigate the impact but also feel as though they lack the time and/or money to do as much as they might like.

The results of that can manifest in any number of ways – beyond the internal burden that depression and anxiety bring. For example, the *My World Survey 2* showed a significant up-tick in the percentage of young adults who reported deliberately hurting themselves – from 22 per cent in 2012 to 33 per cent in 2019. A startling 60 per cent of the 2019 group reported having thought about taking their own life (even though they said they would not do it), compared to 52 per cent in 2012. There was also a slight rise in the numbers who reported making a suicide attempt – 8 per cent compared to 7 per cent.

And while I may have been somewhat glib before about the pressure the housing crisis is bringing to parents compared to their children, it's important to recognise that they are suffering too. Some of them severely. According to Parentline – the parental equivalent of support group Childline – more than 10 per cent of the calls its volunteers now receive are about adult children. Just a few years ago it might have made up around half that proportion.

'The term "walking on eggshells" is so widely used. Immediately, when I hear "adults in the home" I think "walking on eggshells",' says Fiona.

The organisation says it first noticed a significant increase in issues around adult children when Covid-19 struck the country.

Lockdowns saw many adults move back in with their parents for all manner of reasons. But even the ones who were already doing so were suddenly forced to get used to living in much closer quarters than before. And while the pandemic has passed, the issue created by these undesirable living conditions has remained.

Some of the calls to Parentline might seem to be relatively tame – at first glance, at least. There are disagreements around household chores, who gets use of the kitchen at what time and what's put on the sitting room TV. But even at this level, the cumulative effect of troubles can have a significant detrimental effect.

'They're kind of tired of being parents – and they still have that role, and they're still paying bills, and they're still being criticised. A lot of older parents now, who in times past would be enjoying their adult children visiting them, getting on with them, maybe going out with them – and that's changed to feeling responsible for them, worried about them, guilty about the relationship deteriorating to some degree – and then they're annoyed that they're not getting their own life,' says Fiona, who says that some parents are weighed down by the constant snark, hostility and interference they receive from their live-in children.

'Absence makes the heart grow fonder and out of sight, out of mind – but the opposite is true too.'

But while many parents are being denied the opportunity to finally take their reward from raising their children and taking a step back from their hands-on parental duties, others are suffering in far more serious ways. And that tends to crop up more the longer the adult child is stuck in the home.

'That frustration – it gets very, very volatile. There's a lot of violence of adult children towards their parents as they get older – really, they want the parents out of their way,' she says. 'I deal with people where the parents are in the bedroom watching television because they've been told to go to bed early – and these are across all socioeconomic groups; it's not just underprivileged families.'

She says that parents being bullied by adult children has become a common issue – often in the form of verbal abuse and threats, and sometimes through physical violence. Much like domestic abuse involving couples, this dynamic often comes about gradually, with parents spending a long time trying to manage and placate their children before coming to the likes of Parentline for support.

In one case Fiona dealt with, two adult children of a woman moved back home – uninvited – and essentially took over her two-bedroom house. They stayed up late and slept in, and she tried to work around them – keeping herself to her bedroom or the small kitchen, staying quiet in the mornings for fear of waking them up. In another, a stay-at-home son would constantly belittle his mother – from her hobbies to her decor choices – responding to her request to stop smoking in the house by stubbing out his cigarette on the couch she'd just bought and telling her it would be the first thing he'd throw out when she died.

'You just wonder – if anything happened to her would they even be sorry that she's gone or would they think "Great, now we have the house to ourselves". It's quite cruel, really,' she says. 'It's lovely to feel like there's always a place for me at home, but at what point do young adults need to realise "This is my parents' house – this is what they've worked for"?'

In another case, Fiona dealt with a woman who found herself in between her son and some unsavoury characters he owed money to – and had to navigate that while he was stealing money and selling her belongings.

There's probably a myriad of reasons why this issue has grown so significantly in such a short period of time. Some might point to growing substance abuse – particularly in the use of psychotropic drugs. And, as we've already seen, there are growing mental health issues among younger people – which relate to but go beyond the housing market. These are sure to be fuel for this particularly ugly fire.

But it is also no coincidence that the spike in cases handled by the likes of Parentline is mirroring the rise in the number of adult children who are stuck at home. And with no light at the end of the housing tunnel, it is the uncomfortable fact that more families will encounter frustrations, hostilities and even violence unless they can find ways to manage their new dynamic. In the long term, the solution may even be as much about architecture as it is about attitude.

'Dermot Bannon has a lot to answer for,' says Fiona, somewhat jokingly. 'We were all into open plan houses, which was fantastic when you've big families and everyone is running around and everyone is sharing. But then if you've four grown adults living in the house that's open plan, there's no space – and space, your territory, is so important.

'Maybe planning houses for generational living might be the way forward as well – you don't just think of it as a young family home.'

Part V

The Future

Waiting for Death

'Lots of us did', said then Taoiseach Leo Varadkar in January 2018. He was speaking about the practice of would-be first-time buyers hitting up parents for financial help when trying to scrape together a deposit.

It was part of his attempt to outline the various ways that people can – and have always – amassed the funds required to secure a home of their own. But it quickly became a lightning rod for criticism of government housing policy and, in the eyes of its opponents, proof of just how out of touch the country's leadership was. After all, most people don't have the privilege of wealthy parents who can afford to hand over thousands or tens of thousands or even hundreds of thousands of euro to their child (or children). If the remark was to be taken as confirmation that the state intended to rely on the Bank of Mam and Dad to bridge the gap between house prices and earnings, then it was effectively a signal that officialdom was closing the front door on a huge number of wannabe homeowners.

But whether it was by design or default, the Irish housing market has become increasingly reliant on this kind of inter-generational leg-up in recent years. Let's call it a 'Get Out' Dig Out or GODO for short. A 2024 survey by the Banking and Payments Federation Ireland (BPFI) found that nearly 40 per cent of adults had received some kind of a gift and/or inheritance – in most cases from their parents. The vast majority of these GODO gifts came in the form of cash, and a third of those recipients put that cash towards a home.

This tallies with what is happening at the coal face of the housing market. Online mortgage broker doddl.ie reports that around a third of the clients it's working with nowadays have received GODO gifts to help them buy a home – with that proportion rising in recent years. In the vast majority of cases, the average gift was €27,000 – which on its own would go a significant way towards helping the recipient build a decent deposit (especially if you're talking about our Tinderman and his dream of owning a distinctly average home). Meanwhile, for a small number of its gift-getting clients (around 15 per cent), the amount they received was actually in excess of €100,000. And if you break out this 100k+ subset from the rest of the herd, their average GODO gift was actually closer to €200,000. That would go most of the way towards covering the entire cost of an average home, never mind the deposit. (Though even that size of gift pales in comparison to what some others have been given by parents or grandparents. The aforementioned BPFI survey found that, of those who had gotten a gift or inheritance, 22 per cent received it in the form of a dwelling. Who needs deposits or mortgage brokers when you can be just straight-up given a house of your own?)

Now, I don't know about you, but I don't know many people who have a whole house going spare – or €100,000. Or even €27,000. Or, at the very least, if I do know them, they're doing a good job of keeping that information to themselves. But clearly, there are a fair few of them out there. Data from the Central Bank shows that Irish people had a combined €163 billion on deposit at the start of the year – which is a record level of savings. And it doesn't include the billions more locked away in investments. The amount Irish consumers have saved is so significant that, if it was shared out evenly, it would work out at just shy of €40,000 per adult in the country. But herein lies the problem with the market's growing reliance on GODO gifts – because, in reality, all of that money is not shared out evenly. Far from it. The truth is that some savers may have hundreds of thousands of euro on deposit each, while others have nothing. The Bank of Mam and Dad may be a saving grace for many, but it's closed to most. Unfortunately, for a lot of people who are falling short on a deposit, they'll be left waiting for GODO.

Given this, it's understandable that some might try to paint the gifters as the villains of this piece but, in truth, it would be unfair to be too critical of the 'haves' in this very specific case, at least. After all, they (probably) didn't create the housing crisis but they do want to help their children navigate it, and they happen to be in a position to do so. Realistically, there probably aren't many people who would do anything different if they found themselves similarly disposed. That being said, in doing right by their own offspring, this minority group is having a disproportionate, negative impact on everyone else's property purchasing prospects.

The result of all these GODO gifts is that the imbalance that already exists in the housing market is only getting more pronounced. That one-third of doddl.ie clients who have had, on average, tens of thousands of euro gifted to them have an obvious edge over the two-thirds who, presumedly, don't have wealthy parents or grandparents to help them out. That's not even factoring in the many others who haven't even gotten themselves to the position of being taken seriously by a mortgage broker. And all of that extra money – some calculations suggest there are GODO gifts to the value of half a billion euro coursing through the property market each year – is helping to further push up prices. That adds a bigger burden on future buyers' deposit requirements, which makes big gifts even more important to them and puts the gift-less even further behind the starting line as a result.

If this loop continues for too long, it's only a matter of time before the GODO-less are left with no hope at all.

On borrowed time

'It wasn't nice giving up €220,000 at the time but I suppose it relieved a lot of tension in the house here,' says Paddy, a seventy-something retired company director who lives in south Dublin with his wife Paula. They have four kids, all of whom now have places of their own – though one of their daughters has a significant GODO gift to thank for that.

Because, until a few years ago, she had been renting a place while running a successful company of her own – but the pandemic saw her lose both of those things in quick succession. First, lockdown forced her business to close permanently and then, shortly afterwards, her landlord told her she needed to move out. And so she was stranded, out of work and with nowhere to live. She moved back in with her parents, but they decided to offer her a longer-term solution.

'We had a holiday home in Wexford and we sold that a couple of years ago,' says Paddy. 'After paying our taxes and all the rest we had about €220,000 left … so we decided we might help to buy her a house.'

Given that she had been self-employed and was now out of work, getting any kind of mortgage was not on the cards for the daughter – even with the sizeable deposit she'd received from her parents. But given that she had €30,000 of her own from selling off the assets from her defunct business, they hoped there would be enough between them to buy a property outright.

'She was just getting her inheritance early,' Paddy explains – with their three other children set to get their inheritance from the family home after they die. 'We valued our home and we reckon the three other children would get around €230,000 each if it was sold off today.'

And as we've already seen, the kind of impulse felt by Paddy and Paula is fairly normal. Most parents of BROs want to see their child get out and find a place of their own. And, naturally, they'd like to help them in that process.

That might be for altruistic reasons – like wanting to see their offspring strike out on their own and benefit from some long-deserved independence. Maybe it's based on more questionable motives – like their hope of seeing some grandchildren before they're too old to enjoy them. Or maybe they're straight-up selfish and just want their spare room back for … activities. But all reasons are perfectly valid – we listen and we don't judge.

At the same time, a lot of young adults are also hoping for – and even expecting – some kind of a helping hand from their parents. The BPFI survey on gifts and inheritance found that, alongside those who had already received something from their parents or grandparents, a further 35 per cent expected that they would receive a gift and/or inheritance from a relative (most likely their parents) in the future. It's not clear whether that is based on some firm promise made to them or just some over-confident wishful thinking on their part.

But while there are parents who want to help their child out by giving them a GODO gift and a child eagerly waiting to receive one on the other end, not everyone has hundreds of thousands, or even tens of thousands, of euro to hand over to their offspring. And, sometimes, even the ones that do have that kind of money to offer find it's still not enough. But the lack of a chunk of change in the savings account isn't necessarily the end of the story. Within that cohort of people going to banks (and brokers like doddl.ie) with a wedge of their parents' cash in their back pocket, there are some who are doing so despite their parents' lack of savings to hand. Because some have found another way to give a dig out.

That Central Bank savings figure that I mentioned above actually only tells a small part of the story of Irish people's wealth – or their 'on-paper' wealth, at least. Because separate figures from the banks also show that households here have a combined net value of more than €1.2 trillion – which would work out at more than €290,000 per adult in the country. It would include the €163 billion people have saved, but clearly, there's a lot more going on in there beyond that. And, of course, it is the case, once again, that the money is not evenly spread across the country – some households make up far more of that total than others. Though it's probably fair to say that there is a slightly better distribution here than there is in the savings figure because the majority of that household wealth – about two-thirds of it – is from the value of the properties people own.

'You look at reports over the last couple of weeks in terms of Boomers being the most wealthy people in the country – but the reality is that's a balance-sheet view of them. Don't tell them they're wealthy because they don't feel wealthy … if you look at them from a profit and loss view, whatever comes in goes out,' says David Brady, who's a director at Spry Finance.

'They could be in a house that happens to be worth €700,000 because it's in Rathfarnham, but the person living in it is only on €12,000 a year.'

Spry Finance sells 'lifetime loans'.

If you've ever experienced the joy of wasting an afternoon half-watching old episodes of classic quiz shows on some random satellite or cable TV channel, you've probably been given the sales pitch on a lifetime loan a couple of hundred times – from one of the UK's providers at least – although maybe it was referred to at the time as an equity release loan or even a reverse mortgage. But whatever the name, daytime TV is awash with ads for this kind of service.

The basic idea of a lifetime loan is that a homeowner borrows money based on the value of their home – kind of like they would with a mortgage. Unlike a normal loan or mortgage, though, they don't have to make any regular repayments once they get their cash. But, of course, it's not like the lender is handing out free money – it still wants to get paid back. The big difference here is that this tends to happen after the borrower has popped their clogs. After they die, the loan (including the interest that's built up over the months and years) falls due, and it's up to the estate to pay what's owed. The ultimate idea is that some of what's received through the sale of the property will cover whatever is owed.

Given all of that, you can see why the target market for this type of loan tends to be older people who own their own home. They might be the kind of people who don't have much in the way of income (and, as a result, the means to get and repay a regular loan), but they may be sitting on/in a valuable asset. And without wanting to make any sweeping generalisations, you can probably also see why ads for this kind of thing tend to crop up on daytime TV.

It is worth pointing out that the money that people get through the likes of lifetime loans can be put to any number of uses. Maybe the borrower wants to do up their home or refit it to make it easier for them to navigate as they age. Or, perhaps, they want to spend the next few years getting away from their home as often as possible. Or maybe they just need the reassurance of having a financial buffer to hand in case they encounter any major unexpected expenses – like a broken-down boiler or car repairs. And it's these kinds of everyday reasons that tend to explain most of the lending these companies are engaged in – in Ireland at least.

But there's another category that's also a popular reason for borrowing – the GODO gift.

'Some customers are using this as a financial planning tool – they're saying "I'm worth X, I have two kids and they're going to get an inheritance",' says David. 'They have a big plan; it's a transfer of assets – and it's that kind of conversation.'

And it ended up being called upon by Paddy and Paula as they tried to help their daughter secure her own place. Because it turns out that, given the state of the housing market at the moment, even having €250,000 in cash isn't enough to buy a place in the part of Wicklow that they were house-hunting in. This is where they turned to Spry.

'We were able to borrow €100,000 from them. Eventually she managed to get a place for €355,000 – and we're happy, and she's happy, and she's starting a small business again,' he says.

While that loan doesn't have to be paid back until after they die, Paddy and Paula – and their daughter – are paying down the loan now: in part because not doing so could end up eating into their other childrens' inheritance. The fact that it has what Paddy refers to as a 'cruel' interest rate of 6.7 per cent is also an incentive for them to clear it sooner rather than later.

***

According to David from Spry, these kinds of GODO gifts have made up a small but not insignificant part of its lending in recent years. They made up roughly 10 per cent of the money it gave out in 2024.

'From a mom and dad's point of view they're thinking "We're not going anywhere, we've got another 10 to 15 years of really high-quality life, which is great, but you're going to be in your early 50s by the time you get an inheritance – so maybe we can do something for you now."'

And he thinks it will be a bigger part of Spry's loan book in 2025.

'I expect this year to be around 15 per cent of what we lend out – it might even be a little bit more,' he says. 'Property prices don't look like they're going to come down, the government is going to miss housing quotas, there's going to be more pressures around that – so people are going to be looking for solutions.

'Also, we have the longest life expectancy in Europe, which is a good thing … but all of the drivers that might lead someone to do this are there.'

And that's a bigger proportion of a growing loan book. Last year Spry's CEO predicted the value of the lifetime loan market would grow to €200 million a year by 2027. So clearly there is a significant cohort of older people who want to do what they can to help their children get on the property ladder, and they're not letting their own lack of savings act as a barrier to achieving that. It's an admirable desire – though it may not be entirely selfless; David says that some of their applicants are openly motivated by the prospect of finally having a free gaff.

Death watch

While the likes of lifetime loans do offer a solution to a growing problem, they're clearly not for everyone.

Some may, understandably, be uneasy with the idea of taking out a mortgage in their sunset years – even if it doesn't tie them personally to any kind of repayment requirement. Others might not have a property of their own that they can borrow against.

And even among those who have a home and are willing to borrow, there's no guarantee they'll get a loan. Lenders like Spry have eligibility criteria around the likes of the customers' age and the value, location and condition of the property they're basing their loan on. For whatever reason, it may turn out that they're not suitable borrowers anyway.

But, as Spry's own data shows, even if they are willing, able and eligible to tap into the value of their home to get their hands on a chunk of change, there are plenty of other things that retirees might need that money for. So, if someone needs the money to cover the cost of their health and care needs, or if they need to repay loans that were outstanding when they retired, or they want to add a bit of comfort to their lives beyond what the state pension can provide, that's likely going to take priority over padding out their kids' deposits. And lifetime mortgages aren't an unlimited pool customers can tap into – in fact, they're (understandably) relatively restrictive. In Spry's case, it only lends out a maximum of 15 per cent of the property's value, with that cap in place to help protect the borrower and the loan in the event of anything unexpected in the future.

In other words, while some people out there can straight-up gift their kids part or all of a deposit (or a house) and others are happy to take out a loan in order to make that cash available, there are still plenty of young people who are simply not able to bank on the Bank of Mam and Dad.

That means a sizeable segment of the Bailout Babies are at an even bigger disadvantage in their race to get on the ladder. They might be doing what they can to grow their savings, but ever-rising house prices – in part fuelled by wealthy parents and in part fuelled by GODO gifts – mean their deposit target is growing too. They might be hoping to earn their way out of this stasis eventually but, with house price inflation trending well above average salary increases, they'll have to secure one hell of a promotion for that to happen. And, as already mentioned, that's adding to the fact that banks tend to avoid giving out mortgages that still have to be repaid after retirement. So once they hit their 30s, the clock starts ticking and the burden of debt only begins to grow.

So, the longer it takes a Bailout Baby to scrape together a deposit, the more they'll have to borrow to buy a property, and the less time they'll have to repay that. At a certain point the already narrow window they have will simply shut, and whatever prospect they had of getting a mortgage will be gone.

At that stage, what opportunity is left open to them that might allow them to get on the property ladder? Are they going to have to live in hope of a lotto win in order to buy their own place? Or – perhaps more realistically – are they just going to have to wait around for their parents to die and hope there's enough left in the will to get them to homeowner status?

The retired renter

Your parents' demise being your best hope of getting a home of your own is sure to be a pretty uncomfortable thought (for most people, anyway). But so too is the idea of simply never getting on the property ladder – because homeownership is an intrinsic part of being Irish. Much like being up for the craic, enjoying the grand stretch and supporting whatever team is playing against England, buying a house is simply an unspoken part of Ireland's social contract. And the extent of that expectation makes us quite different to most of the countries we like to compare ourselves to. It's not like owning a home is uncommon in other countries – but the European outlook is far more amendable towards renting indefinitely; in Ireland, it's generally assumed that renters are just temporarily hindered homeowners.

Through the years there have been plenty of theories put out there to explain why that is. The most common ones build on the idea that, having had our homes and possessions stolen by our colonial oppressors and having been denied property ownership for generations, we now have an almost genetic predisposition to getting and holding onto whatever patch of land we can find now that doing such a thing is a possibility once again. As it goes, that colonial oppression also happens to be the obvious explanation for why we have an innate love of seeing English teams lose.

But while our intergenerational trauma may well have been a foundational factor in our love of land – and possibly still is a factor to this day – there are arguably many more practical reasons for our ongoing yearning for homeownership. Because our housing market is not designed with renting in mind and – despite decades of growing demand – it has not adapted to become so, there is a continual shortage of rental properties and a relatively narrow scope for the type of renters that might exist. Meanwhile there continues to be a lack of security of tenure in the market, with renters knowing they may be months or even weeks away from being turfed out of their current home. And issues like this have been major contributory factors towards the high cost – with monthly rents far exceeding the mortgage that would be due on a similar property.

At the same time so much of our economic and social system is built around the assumption that, whatever else you have when you retire, you at least have your own home. As we've already seen, for many it is far and away the most valuable asset they hold upon retirement. In fact, in a lot of cases, it is the only real asset they have to their name. A retiree having their own home is clearly an expectation held by the state – with the rate of the national pension priced on the assumption that the recipient doesn't have a large monthly mortgage or rent bill to worry about in addition to their regular food and utility expenses. And should an older person need to enter a nursing home at any stage, but not have the cash to fund that directly, the state's solution is once again built on the assumption of homeownership. The HSE's Fair Deal scheme lets someone offer up a portion of their home to cover some of the cost. And the idea here is that, similarly enough to the Spry Finance model, the value of that share will likely get paid back to the HSE after the patient dies.

The problem here is clear. If we end up with a generation that simply could not work their way into homeownership, these systems – and the state's social safety net in general – will quickly come under significant pressure. And that is exactly what's predicted to happen if we stay on our current course.

A 2022 report by the ESRI found that, at the moment, around 90 per cent of over 65s own their own home. Of the minority that do not, most are in some form of state-supported accommodation rather than the private rental market. But the ESRI predicts that, of those currently in their mid-30s to mid-40s, just 65 per cent are likely to retire as homeowners. That represents a huge shift from the current norm and leaves a significant minority of this generation facing retirement as renters. And, given the fact that housing pressures are growing over time rather than receding, it's worse still for those aged 25 to 34. While the ESRI notes that there is greater uncertainty around any predictions it might make for these people – in part due to the difficulty of forecasting their future earnings prospects – it suggests around half of them could retire without their own home.

It's not hard to imagine the personal and societal challenges this would create. All things being equal, a retired renter who is reliant on the state pension (as around half of workers are currently expected to be) will naturally struggle to cover rent as well as their basic living needs. The only way that changes is if there's a significant drop in the cost of rent in the coming decades or a significant increase in the state pension (and maybe both would be needed to actually make this situation work). The retiring renter would also be locked out of the likes of the Fair Deal scheme, if they eventually needed nursing home care, and be unable to raise any lump sums that they might need through companies like Spry. And this will inevitably push more people towards the breadline.

The ESRI report says that, currently, around 14 per cent of retirees are classed as having income poverty after their housing costs are factored in. But this could rise to as much as 31 per cent in the future as homeownership rates among this cohort decline. This would only increase the number of people reliant on state supports – from the state pension, to additional social welfare payments, to state-owned accommodation. And with a third – and eventually as much as half – of these people predicted to be retiring without a home, that would ultimately represent a dramatic increase in pressure on the public coffers.

Either that or we quickly learn to get comfortable with the even more regular sight of homeless and destitute pensioners.

Eggs, SINKS and DINKS

We're usually quite good at celebrating the areas where the Irish punch above our weight. Award nominations are treated the same way other countries might react to wins. World Cup quarter finals appearances are almost as revered here as an actual trophy is in others (in soccer at least). Our Eurovision song contest legacy is a thing of countrywide pride – even among people who hate the actual song contest. But one area of our over-achieving that has tended to be under-celebrated is our knack for having children. Because even way back in the depths of our economic malaise, when we struggled with everything from growing our agricultural output to mastering industrial manufacturing, we were world class when it came to making babies. And that's not just a stereotype based on the (many) dodgy portrayals of mucky-faced Irish families in American and British media; nor is it an anecdotal assumption born of the fact that we all have at least one grandparent with siblings in the double digits. Ireland's procreational prowess is a statistical fact.

Data from the European Commission on the region's fertility rate through the decades shows this quite clearly. In the 1970s, birth rates indicated that the likes of the Danes, Finns, Swedes, Austrians and Belgians were managing to have an average of around two children per woman (this is the basis for what's known as the total fertility rate, which tells you how many children the average woman would have based on the number of births in any given year). But, at the same time, the women of Ireland were managing an average of almost four children each (which actually seems kind of low based on the anecdotal evidence we all have about how many siblings our parents, grandparents and great-grandparents had). And Ireland's impressive perinatal performance continued into the 1980s. Because while this decade saw the women of wider Europe tending to have two kids or fewer, the Irish were hitting a rate of more than three chizzlers per woman.

But the fact that our out-performance isn't exactly a source of national pride may be based on the reality that this remarkable productivity was not just poverty-stricken – it was poverty-fuelled too. That's because data from around the world, and through the decades, consistently shows a correlation between weaker economic development and a high fertility rate. And while a poor person creating more dependants might seem counter-productive, it is actually argued to be a direct consequence of it, as families attempt to improve their economic lot. The logic is that having more children means bringing more potential future labourers, workers and earners into the household. (In the case of Ireland, they may also be future émigrés who will send money back home to fund the running of the house.) Over the longer term, that small army of kids can then also act as a kind of pension fund for those unable to build a more traditional kind of retirement fund that would otherwise ensure them a comfortable dotage.

Of course, that's not to say that Ireland's high fertility rate was purely an act of economic desperation. There are plenty of other factors behind our advanced virility, religion being just one of them. After all, people may have been procreating to profit in the long run – but the fact that, in the Ireland of old, a condom was harder find than a job only served to intensify the trend.

However, the global data that links poverty to population growth also tells us that as a country becomes wealthier its fertility rate tends to decline. That's believed to happen because there's no longer a need to have a large family in order to bring more money into the household. At the same time having more women enter the workforce butts up against any desire they (or the society around them) may have for them to become stay-at-home babymakers. Meanwhile improving educational standards also tends to mean a better awareness of the nuances of effective family planning.

And this is exactly what happened to Ireland once we hit the economic jackpot. Because, as the country shifted from the doldrums of the 1980s and into the Celtic Tiger era of the 1990s, our fertility rate also began to fall off its lofty perch. From having more than three children a piece in the early 1980s, birth rates tell us that the average Irish woman was having a whole child less by the start of 1990s – with the fertility rate dipping from 3.21 children to 2.11 in the space of a decade. By European standards that was still high – it was above the average, at least – but Ireland was no longer the massive offspring outlier that it once was. In fact, the sudden shift meant that Ireland was no longer Europe's top of the pops in terms of popping out sprogs, with Cyprus and Sweden suddenly outdoing us on that front.

Interestingly, though, following that sharp drop in the space of a decade, our fertility rate pretty much levelled out from that point on, at least for the next 20 years or so. In fact, it bounced around that kind of range of two-ish-per-woman from 1990 all the way through to around 2012. That indicates that, while the arrival of money into the country saw us rethink our collective family plans and cut back somewhat on our human output, we found a new equilibrium at two children each. And given the length of time for which it held steady, you'd be forgiven for thinking that the new rate was almost immovable – after all, it wasn't affected by the excess and opportunity of the boomiest moments of the boom, or the fear and loathing of the crashiest moments of the crash.

But it wasn't immovable – it's just that this time it took a housing crisis, rather than prosperity, to knock back our knocking up.

From 2013 onwards the rate began to move downwards once again and it's been stuck on a sharply negative path ever since. Having been having babies at a rate of more than two per woman in 2012, it fell to 1.93 in 2013, then 1.8 in 2017 and then 1.7 in 2022. By 2023, it was a rate of just 1.5 children per woman. It's a dramatic shift in the space of a decade – and in ways, it's more significant than the one that was seen between the 1980s and 1990s because it means that Ireland has now, quite rapidly, found itself well short of the so-called 'replacement rate' of 2.1 – that's the somewhat cold-blooded name that economists have for the minimum number of babies that need to be born each year in order to ensure they are replacing the people who have died.

At 1.5 children per woman, Ireland's rate is also shifting rapidly towards what's called 'lowest-low fertility'.

A look under the parent-hood

Of course, broad averages like fertility rates are only going to tell you so much. To fully understand what's happening with Ireland's personal productivity, you need to look a little closer.

First and foremost, there are fewer births in Ireland today than was the case just a few years ago. In 2023, there were fewer than 54,700 births – which represents a more than 20 per cent decrease on the number 10 years before. And this is coming at a time of population growth, which immediately explains why the fertility rate slipped by half a child in the same period.

And one of the biggest contributing factors behind that is the fact that women here are having babies later in life than ever before.

Back in 1973, the average age of first-time mothers was 25. By 2003, the average age had shifted to just over 28 – a remarkably modest change given all that had happened economically and socially in the country during those three decades. Fast-forward another 10 years and a first-time mother's average age was just over 30 – and by 2023, it had moved on again to 31.6. A large part of the catalyst for that is a notable decline in the number of births by women in their 20s and 30s, especially in the past decade. Among women aged 20 to 24 it has declined by around three-quarters, while births amongst those aged 25 to 29 were down by more than a third. In fact, the only age categories to have seen numbers of births increase between 2013 and 2023 are those aged 40 to 44, and those aged 45 and over.

There are some contributory factors to this that most people would see as positive. For example, the slip in the average age of mothers overall is partially explained by the fact that there has been a huge dip in the number of teens giving birth – with the 2023 figure nearly 75 per cent lower than it was in 2003. At the same time, women today are, generally, more willing and able to prioritise their careers and lives over the idea of having children – and so they are delaying their maternal moment as a result. The widespread availability and general social acceptance of contraceptives will have had a not-insignificant impact too.

But while many are making a conscious decision to put off having children, others have now become trapped as Postponed Parents as an uninvited consequence of their circumstances.

A February 2025 survey for the Catholic counselling service Accord found that, among couples aged 25 to 34, 60 per cent of those who wanted children had not taken that particular step due to their housing situation. A third of them said they would have had a child in the past three years but hadn't because they wanted to secure a home first. And it's not like they were holding out for some idealised notion of the perfect nuclear family. Because in Ireland, unlike many other countries, the rental market is an unreliable and unpredictable one with no guarantee, or even expectation, of long-term tenure. As we've already discussed, multi-year leases are the norm in continental European countries – and there is even an expectation that tenants will furnish and decorate 'their' place – all while the Irish system is very much a year-by-year roulette wheel. Not to mention the even more practical reality that having a child is counted against you in a mortgage application – denting the amount a bank will be willing to lend you. It makes sense on many levels to try and have your mortgage in the bag first – and you can think about the offspring afterwards.

And the Postponed Parents that this survey shines a light on are probably only the tip of the iceberg in terms of the numbers of people who might already have had kids were it not for their lack of housing, because it was very much focused on committed couples who were long past the crucial 'where is this relationship going?' benchmark – some respondents were already engaged and likely in the midst of saving for a place of their own. But, of course, there are many other committed couples today who have no plans whatsoever to get married – and many others who may plan to but just not through the Catholic Church. But the others who are unseen by this survey statistic are those who are not yet at that point in their lives – again, due to circumstances outside of their control. Because, as we have already learned, the housing crisis is having an impact at the ground zero of coupling up – it's making it harder for people to meet partners in the first place and then develop the relationship into something serious enough to be at the 'where is this relationship going?' stage. That has created a hidden demographic of young singletons who might otherwise have reached – or passed – the babymaking stage of their relationship were it not for their housing situation.

Now, this, of course, is all a bit of a 'what if'. Some of the people in this group might not even realise that they are in this group. As a result, it's pretty much impossible to calculate the size of this demographic. Despite that, there are still ways in which the growing group of Postponed Parents are becoming visible.

Eggs, baskets

When I'm told I'm about to get a look at the cryostore, I already have a clear mental image of what that will look like. I see myself walking into a vast, cold building that's decked out with aisles and aisles of stainless-steel compartments that stretch from floor to ceiling – almost like some kind of futuristic library. Staff, dressed head to toe in PPE, walk through and carefully check digital displays, noting the readings on their tablets. Wisps of water vapour from the gallons of liquid nitrogen blanket the white tiled floor.

It turns out my mental image is a tiny bit off-target.

It turns out the cryostore, in this case at least, looks more like a mid-sized utility room. There are no aisles of stainless-steel containers but, instead, a small number of white tanks lined up along the wall … imagine those yellow gas canisters you'd use with a barbecue but a good bit bigger. There is liquid nitrogen – though there are no wisps to be seen as it's all very well contained inside a large tank that sits in the middle of the room. (The liquid nitrogen tank is stainless steel, though, so I get a point for that.)

While the reality of Beacon Fertility's cryostore doesn't quite live up to the picture that Hollywood had created for me, it still represents the cutting edge of fertility technology. And as small as the room may be compared to my expectations, it's capable of catering to thousands of patients.

As Dr Ahmed Omar, medical director at Beacon Fertility explains to me, 'an embryo is about the size of a small grain of salt – and an egg can't be seen with the naked eye.'

Which is handy, because demand for the facility's services – and in particular its egg-freezing service – has grown dramatically in recent years. In the past three years alone, I'm told the number of clients who have frozen eggs has trebled, with single women making up a significant proportion.

'They might go and have a baby, or two [naturally] – but when they are in their late 30s or early 40s they might get into a bit of difficulty – so I think this is still, for the long term, a good plan for them,' he says.

It's a similar story at Sims IVF, another one of the country's leading fertility service providers. It has seen a 300 per cent increase in the number of egg-freezing patients over the past seven years.

'We've seen a significant change post-Covid compared to pre-Covid,' says Dr Carolina Tovar, who is Senior Fertility Consultant in the Sims IVF clinic in south Dublin. 'There were very stable numbers of egg-freezing before Covid, then it doubled after Covid and we've steadily seen an increase of approximately 20 to 25 per cent of cycles each year since then.

'So, it's huge, the difference.'

Egg-freezing isn't a particularly new thing, with versions of it being used as far back as the 1980s. However, it was traditionally a far less successful 'assisted reproductive' method than freezing embryos or even sperm, with less than half of all eggs tending to survive the freezing and thawing process. As a result, for most of its history it tended to be offered as a last resort to patients with little else to lose – for example, cancer patients going through chemotherapy.

'Freezing eggs was mainly an option for oncology patients that don't have any time – so this was as best as we can do to preserve your options for the future,' she says. 'But in the past, we didn't use egg-freezing for social reasons – but we do now.'

The change that came in the early 21st century was a far more successful fast-freezing approach, which has grown to become the standard over the past 15-or-so years. As a result of that, now the vast majority of eggs survive – from a less-than-50-per-cent survival rate to around 85 per cent. That means the service is no longer the preserve of the desperate. At the same time, the idea itself has come into the mainstream consciousness far more, with the likes of Jennifer Aniston talking about her regret over not freezing eggs and encouraging young women not to make the same mistake.

'Our phones were off the hook after she said that,' says Annmarie Cullen, head of marketing at Beacon Fertility.

At the same time, a string of big tech and finance companies – from Spotify to Apple to Goldman Sachs – have gradually announced that they would cover the cost of the process for their employees, something they proudly pitched as part of their ever-increasing efforts to encourage diversity and inclusion in the workplace. (Although, if they thought the move would garner them some positive PR they were sadly mistaken. It ultimately backfired, with critics claiming that their egg-freezing offer was less to do with diversity and more to do with dividends – as they saw the move as a thinly veiled attempt by companies to yield more control over their employees' lives. Why waste the prime years of your life having babies, they seemed to be saying, when you could instead focus all of that energy on boosting your bosses' bottom line?)

But while the tech itself (and the big-tech employers) may have made egg-freezing more accessible, the shifting sands of young people's prospects are undeniably playing a part in its growing popularity, because it is taking them longer than ever to reach the 'ideal' moment to try for a baby – whatever that may actually mean. As we've already discussed, there are obviously many factors behind this delay – including the fact that women are spending more time in education and focusing their efforts on building a career. But both Dr Omar and Dr Tovar separately say housing is a factor – as it is pushing back the age at which people are ready to try for a baby, which in turn is increasing their chances of needing fertility assistance. And that's reflected in that Accord/Amárach survey, which shows that the majority are delaying some of life's major landmarks in order to first secure a home (the survey also says that women are more likely to do so than men). Meanwhile, we've seen how younger people are having a harder time starting relationships in the first place – and moving those relationships along into something serious.

So, clearly, in more ways than one, the housing crisis is playing a significant and increasing role in our dwindling birth rate.

At the same time, the rise in egg-freezing specifically indicates a growth in the number of would-be mothers who currently remain outside of a serious relationship – because if they were in one, but still looking to delay pregnancy for whatever reason, they'd be better off with the slightly more reliable method of freezing an embryo rather than an egg. And so, aware of the issues that can arise, they are creating a Plan B for themselves.

'I feel like, for me, if I had left it any longer, I could be in a position where I have nothing – so, I want some reassurance,' says Sorcha, who's 31 now but started freezing her eggs at 28.

She started working for Sims IVF three years ago but had no background in fertility before then. And while she wants to have kids in the future, she reckoned that – at 28, in good health – time was on her side.

'You're told as a girl growing up, if your cycles are regular and you don't have painful periods, you'll be grand – you'll be able to have kids and it won't be any bother.'

And so, she had no intention of freezing her eggs either until curiosity about the area she was working in got the better of her.

'One day I was here and I decided I was going to see what my fertility was like … and I got my results and it was really, really bad,' she says. 'Say the range for my age group was 15 to 30 – mine was down at 1. So really, really low.'

The advice she was given was not to sit on the results and wait – because as hard as it may be to conceive now, it will only get harder as she gets older. But at the time, she didn't have a partner and was instead focused on the Herculean effort of getting onto the property ladder on a single income. And so, she opted to freeze her eggs.

But that's not to say it's an easy route. Far from it.

It's an expensive process, for a start. Providers like Sims IVF and Beacon Fertility charge around €3,000 for an egg-harvesting cycle. One may be enough to produce a decent sample but, if not, additional cycles – also costing thousands of euro – may be required. And there is an annual charge for the storage of the eggs, too.

It's also more of a process than a simple procedure. To harvest their eggs a patient first needs to go on a course of hormones to stimulate their ovaries and, assuming that's successful and the conditions are just right, a long, thin needle – guided by an ultrasound – is inserted into their vaginal wall and the egg or eggs are retrieved. It's at this point that they are fast-frozen – and stored away until they are needed.

'You have to be aware of your physical wellbeing – because it takes a lot out of you. You're doing the hormone injections and going through a lot in a short period of time. And the second is your mental wellbeing; you really do need to take care of that while you go through something like this. Because it is a lot,' says Sorcha.

The doctors at both Beacon Fertility and Sims IVF caution that there is no guarantee when it comes to egg-freezing – or with any form of fertility treatment. They have also both had only limited demand for the eggs to be thawed so far.

'Let's say 10 to 15 per cent of patients will come back to use those eggs,' says Dr Tovar. 'And those that come back are usually the ones who froze their eggs when they were older … and they are not the patients that have the most optimal results.'

The fact that there are fewer, older patients retrieving their eggs is in part because of how niche the service was just a few years ago. In some cases, it's because the women managed to conceive naturally – so they haven't needed to revert to their Plan B. In many cases, though, it's because the women have still not gotten themselves into that 'ideal' position of having a house and a stable partner.

Marisa Tomei stamps her foot on a cabin porch

It's not just with regard to egg-freezing that Beacon Fertility and Sims IVF have seen an increase in demand. That ever-slipping age at which women have their first child means that there are a lot more people encountering the kinds of fertility issues that tend to go hand in hand with getting older. And, as Dr Omar tells me, it's not always straight away – some will have little to no issues conceiving their first child but, when they decide to try and give them a sibling two or three years down the line, things have changed.

'We're seeing a lot of what we call secondary infertility – it's not the difficulty of having your first baby but maybe your second or third sometimes – because of the age factor,' he says.

And it stands to reason – given that there is a ticking clock in all of this (for women at least) – that having older first-time mothers will inevitably lend itself to there being smaller families in general. And so it goes. According to the CSO, the average number of children per family in the country was 1.34 on the night of Census 2022. That marks a gradual decline on the 2016 figure, which was itself down slightly on the 2011 figure. It is a significant fall, though, on the 1996 average of 1.82 – in other words a 26 per cent decline over two and a half decades.

And given the nature of what we're talking about, it also has to be remembered that any change at 'ground zero' would take many years to 'wash' through. After all, even if all young couples stopped having children altogether right now, there are still the many families that already exist that would keep the average up for years to come. With that in mind, the average number of children-per-family falling by a quarter in 26 years is arguably a dramatic shift.

What's causing that is a little clearer from some separate Census data – which gives a picture of what's underneath the changes in average family size … and the cause might not be what you think.

Between 2011 and 2022, the number of families with four children fell – while all other categories grew. But the total number of families in the country also increased in that time – by around 100,000 to 1.28 million – and so you have to adjust the numbers to get a clearer picture of what's going on. When you do that, you see that the percentage of family units with four children or more went from around 5.5 per cent in 2011 to 4.5 per cent in 2022. At the same time, there was an increase in the number of three-child families – to the tune of 12,690. When the overall growth is accounted for, they continued to make up 12.3 per cent of all families. The number of two-child families grew by 37,844 in the period – which represented a slight increase (bringing them to more than a quarter of all families as opposed to 24.2 per cent in 2011). And while one-child families grew by 7,342, that meant they actually made up a smaller percentage of all families by 2022 (27.1 per cent compared to 28.8 per cent).

But the biggest influence on the falling child-per-family average actually has nothing to do with children. Because over the 11-year period there were 49,108 more families without any children at all. That's by far the biggest increase in real terms; it also represents the biggest upward shift in percentage terms, with this group accounting for 30.8 per cent of families in 2022 compared to 29.2 per cent in 2011. Some of these figures will be due to the increased numbers of Postponed Parents who we've already spoken about.

'One thing that has happened over the past 10 years has been a very marked drop in fertility – and some of that can be put down to what is going in the housing market and around childcare,' says

Prof. Edgar Morgenroth of the Dublin City University (DCU) Business School in Dublin. 'Both of them are expensive and, for some people, it's just not affordable to have kids.'

However, alongside those who are priced out of parenthood there is another, more deliberate movement that is bumping up the childless family number – the one made up of voluntary SINKs and DINKs.

Getting that SINKing feeling

They've been talking about DINKs – and SINKs – for decades.

Standing for 'Double Income, No Kids' (and, as you might have already worked out, 'Single Income, No Kids'), the acronyms seem to have first emerged in the 1980s, though the exact point of origin is unclear. At the time, they were applied to the kind of young, upwardly mobile professionals who were too busy building careers – and enjoying their newfound wealth – to consider settling down into a life of domesticity. And the terms – and the air of disdain that often comes with them – have hung around for most of the intervening years ('Couples having too good a time to have children' read an *Irish Independent* headline from 28 August 2003).

But the terms have found a new lease of life in the past decade, both in Ireland and around the world, as the numbers to which they can apply continue to grow. And their increased significance is evidenced by the fact that a whole dictionary of supporting acronyms has cropped up around them. You might not just be a DINK – you could be a DINKWAD (Double Income, No Kids, With Dog). Even if you're a SINK, you might not be happy about that – which could make you a SINBAD (Single Income, No Boyfriend, Absolutely Desperate). Meanwhile, if you're a SINK who's trying to tap up the Bank of Mam and Dad, then you're probably also a KIPPER (Kids in Parents' Pockets Eroding Retirement Savings). And those put-upon parents are also PODWOGs (Parents of DINKs Without Grandchildren).

And you thought I was pushing my luck with 'BROs'.

But as absurd as the attached acronym soup may be, it does point to the growth – and growing complexity – of the child-free demographic. And while SINKs and DINKs are not automatically opposed to procreation – some could be hoping that the 'no kid' bit is temporary – there is also a growing number of people who are 'childfree by choice'.

The exact extent of the movement in Ireland is hard to gauge accurately because there is – as things stand – an extremely limited amount of research on this demographic in this country. It is also fair to say that, however big the club is, not all of its members made their choice based on their finances. One of the few pieces of relevant Irish research on this – by psychotherapist Deirdre O'Keeffe as part of her masters at DCU – found that some were child-free because they feared the physical and mental toll a child would have on them, some were put off by the loss of freedom, while others simply had no strong urge to propagate. In research in other countries, some have cited their existential dread around the future of the planet – and even the carbon impact of children – as their reason for ending their bloodline.

But finances do play their role because – while the PR department for Babies Inc. may try to tell you otherwise – having children is a major monetary decision. December 2024 research by the ERSI found that households with children had the highest expenditure needs of any of the groups studied ('Well, duh,' says the chorus of people with kids). The report said that, as a result of that, these households were one of the groups most likely to have outgoings higher than their income (renters were another cohort that were more at risk of not having the income to cover costs – so that's a double whammy for those Struggling with Children And Rent … which could make for another catchy acronym). An October 2024 survey of US consumers found that DINKs were saving twice as much each month as those with a double income and kids (I guess they're just DIKs?), and were four times as likely to say they had no financial stress.

And really, you don't even need to have a child – or be reading up on the latest research around familial finances – to understand the financial impact a child will have. If you're already struggling to cover your own cost of living, then, of course, the introduction of a freeloading baby is only going to make that harder. While there may once have been a time in Ireland when having a child was seen as a way of improving your financial lot, now it's very much the opposite.

The Baby Bust

The Bailout Babies are a ticking time bomb.

Not psychologically. Well, not necessarily. Though given that they're continually denied the perks of the supposed social contract despite years of struggling, striving and hustling, that's not exactly something you can rule out either.

But, putting all of those pesky emotions to one side for a minute and looking at things purely from a cold-eyed, biological balance-sheet sort of perspective, there is a major demographic problem brewing within this up-coming generation. To explain it, it might be best to first take a step back and look at another demographic problem that is already widely reported.

The pensions time bomb – or pensions crisis, as it's sometimes, less dramatically, referred to – is the population shift that is set to place significant pressure on the country's public pension system. That's because our state pension isn't paid for through some massive pile of savings that we, as a country, have set aside – it's covered through our current Exchequer income. That means that some of the taxes today's workers are paying are going directly into the pockets of pensioners. And when there are numerous workers working for every pensioner that's pensioning, the system runs fairly smoothly. But if the number of pensioners increases – and the number of workers-per-pensioner declines, it becomes a problem. And that's what is happening in Ireland.

In fairness, this pensions crisis is being faced by many countries, to a greater or lesser extent. But the challenge is particularly acute in Ireland for a number of reasons. This country was once the young man of Europe – thanks in no small part to how productive our mothers, grandmothers and great-grandmothers were back in the day. Our young workforce was one of the factors that allowed the Celtic Tiger to be quite as strong as it was. But now we're ageing. Rapidly.

In 2011, the median age in Ireland was 34 – by 2022, that had risen to 38.3. Ireland had one of the biggest upward shifts in average age between 2013 and 2023 (rising by 3.7 years, compared to the EU average of 2.3 years). By 2024, we were still, just about, holding on to our 'young buck of Europe' status – though that's increasingly like bragging that you're the youngest guy in the bingo hall. At the same time, we're living far longer than ever before and longer than our European brethren. The average life expectancy at birth in 2021 was 80.5 for a man and 84.3 for a woman; 3.3 years and 1.4 years above the EU average, respectively. These figures are also a significant improvement on our historical averages. Just over a decade ago, average life expectancy stood at 78.4 for men and 82.8 for women. And that was a sizeable improvement on the figures in 1991, when an average man would have expected to live to 72.3 and a woman might have made it to 77.9 years old. That's undeniably a good thing – we're living healthier lives, while medical advances have given us a better chance of avoiding and surviving serious illnesses. But it also means we're all going to be spending a lot more time taking money out of the state coffers.

'Our state pension and our civil service pension, we don't really save for them,' says Prof. Edgar Morgenroth of the DCU School of Business. 'We pay for this from current income – and if you've got an ageing population with a constant retirement age – if they all retire at 65 or 66 – at some point the group of people who are in the labour force, who are working, who are paying their taxes to pay for the pensions – that group will shrink.'

When you combine a shrinking working population with more pensioners who are living longer, that will leave us with far fewer workers to fund retirees. It's estimated that, at the moment, there are 4.5 workers for every one pensioner in the country. By 2050, that ratio is expected to fall to just two workers to cover each person with a pension.

There's no shortage of proposals on how best to address this – from raising the age at which someone can claim a pension, to raising taxes on the workers of today to help plug the gap. It's fair to say, though, that few of these ideas are particularly popular. But with an estimated 40 per cent of private workers expected to be solely reliant on the state pension at the time of their retirement, something's got to give. In recent times, by way of a fix, the government has sought to introduce a pensions auto-enrolment scheme in order to strongly persuade people to build up an extra nest egg for their dotage – though the starting date for that has been continually pushed back. Meanwhile, some of the surplus corporation tax take has been earmarked for a sovereign wealth fund that will 'support' state expenditure in the decades ahead. Growing global trade tensions cast a doubt on just how much of a surplus will actually be available for this Future Ireland Fund – but even if it does all go to plan, it won't resolve the issue.

'It's not going to be enough, no,' says Prof. Morgenroth. 'It's a good thing to do but we've had money put away before and then the financial crisis hit and the money was very quickly gone – and that's why I worry about downturns; they have a habit of eating whatever you put away very, very quickly. And you still are left with the problems that you identified quite some time ago.'

And that's just the challenge posed by the already widely recognised pensions crisis. It's fair to say that the Bailout Babies' demographic deluge has the potential to be far more significant.

And as we've already learned, an inability to get a place of their own is having a cascade effect on this generation. It's making it harder to form and develop meaningful relationships, which is delaying them finding a mate, which is further postponing the day they can escape their parents' box room. And that's leading them to push back any plans they have to start a family of their own, which is ultimately leading them to have fewer (if any) children

Ireland's birth rate was already rapidly falling towards the EU average and the CSO's current assumption is that Ireland's fertility rate will continue to fall in the coming decade – reaching the 'lowest-low' rate of 1.3 by 2037 and remaining there for the years ahead. But given the numerous pressure points on would-be parenthood, even that may be a tad optimistic.

In other words, even the most sober analysis sees the flow of new, young workers slowing in the years to come – but there is a chance that the production line may decline to a trickle.

At the same time, the people who are already born can look forward to far longer lives than those enjoyed by previous generations – building on the improvements we've already seen in our life expectancy. The CSO predicts that mortality will improve every year over the next three decades, raising a man's life expectancy from 80.2 in 2022 to 86.2 in 2057 and a woman's from 83.9 in 2022 to 89.1 in 2057. Good news for birthday candle makers, bad news for pensions planners. It means that, as things stand, an average retiree in 2057 may look forward to more than 20 years of pensions payments (or 23 if they're a woman) – all somehow funded by the taxes of just two workers. Let's hope they work in tech.

'Economists have done a fair bit of work on this over the years – it's ultimately going to increase the tax burden for the younger generations. Not having kids makes that worse, because they will be wanting a pension at some point as well,' says Prof. Morgenroth. 'I might be next in line looking for my son to pay my pension, but his generation will be looking for a pension too at some point – so it gets even worse if we don't deal with it.'

But as we've also learned, the financial pressures on the future retirees of the Bailout Baby generation look set to be far greater than the ones facing the pensioners of today. While the state pension may not be described by many as overly generous, it likely provides a manageable day-to-day income for most – but that's only if they're not having to use some or all of it to cover their rent. Yet that is something that a growing percentage of our growing pensioner population will likely have to do in the decades to come. And as more and more of today's unmortgaged population find themselves ageing out of banks' risk models – like a sprinter trying to keep sight of the sundown – that proportion is only likely to grow further. The end result of that is that the equivalent of today's state pension simply won't be enough for them to stay above water. Those two workers will have to start doing overtime.

And, by definition, those house-less retirees will be more vulnerable too. Not only will they have to figure out how to make their basic pension cover their rent and other outgoings, they'll have little to no way of building up a buffer for any unexpected expenses. They won't have the asset of their own house to leverage into cash through the likes of an equity release loan, nor will they be able to offer a piece of the property as collateral for any nursing home move that they may need to make. They will become even more reliant on the state – and charity – to keep them fed, watered and warm. They won't even be able to take a page from their ancestors' book and rely on their cash-cow kids – because they won't have had any. I wonder how those two workers feel about double shifts …

If the drift continues, the ripples of the housing crisis could ultimately build into a perilous predicament for the country. And that's not catastrophising – it's already happening elsewhere.

Seoul mate

Ireland and South Korea may not seem like the most obvious bedfellows – they are two very different countries, with different cultures, climates and outlooks. But there are more than a few parallels all the same.

Both have histories that carry the scars of colonial oppression and both have been shaped (quite literally) by the resulting partition. Both initially struggled with antiquated economies, while large families were the norm (the average Korean woman had six children in the 1960s). Both countries invested in education as a route out of their respective economic malaise and both saw the fruits of that in the form of rapid economic expansion. South Korea was even branded as one of the so-called 'Asian Tigers', the term that eventually inspired the name of our own economic 'miracle'.

And today, both Ireland and South Korea operate open, trade-, tech- and finance-focused economies – and both are in rude health.

But behind the veil of its solid GDP, South Korea is facing a major demographic crisis – one that makes Ireland's falling birth rate look like a baby boom. The country's fertility rate last stood at the so-called 'replacement rate' of 2.1 back in the mid-1980s – just a few years before Ireland's fell to the same benchmark. But while Ireland's has fallen steadily from that point on, South Korea's has slipped into relative free-fall – hitting a historical low of 0.72 in late 2024. The situation is so dire that, if the birth rate stays the same in the coming years, the country's population will halve by the early 2080s. And, by that time, over 65s will make up nearly 60 per cent of the population – with just over 0.6 workers for every pensioner. Our two double-shifting workers don't know how lucky they have it.

Of course, the reason for this fall is complex – and part of it boils down to the same trend of modernisation and economic growth that pushed Ireland's fertility rate down. But experts cite housing as a key component in South Korea's declining births, particularly when it comes to the sharp fall that's been seen in the past decade.

A steep rise in rental prices in the mid-2010s, followed by a jump in house prices, made it harder for young people to get their own place – and start their own families. And attempts by the government to address this at the time, like increasing the amount buyers could borrow, only pushed prices higher.

In the space of just five years, from 2015 to 2020, the country's fertility rate fell from 1.24 to 0.84.

And the risks that this decline pose are hard to understate – with some commentators talking in very real terms about the potential for the country to slip into a terminal decline. Because if you have a dwindling supply of young people, demand for schools and universities falls too. Demand for retail, groceries and cafés will fall too, and all kinds of companies will ultimately struggle to fill jobs, eventually leading to an across-the-board decline in business activity. Fewer workers also means less income and sales-related taxes – and lower economic activity means a decline in the likes of corporation tax. But, at the same time that that's happening, demand for state support will be rising – because of the ever-increasing number of retirees. It's estimated that the cost of health, long-term care and pensions could double in South Korea by 2060.

The lesson here for Ireland is quite clear – it is not a given that people will continue to start families of their own no matter their circumstances. There is a point at which the hurdles – even for those who desperately want to have children – become too high. And if that happens *en masse* it won't just be a hard luck story for the individuals involved, it will be an existential problem for all of us.

'Fertility is down below replacement – if you don't have non-Irish people coming to Ireland, then the population would be declining,' says Prof. Morgenroth. 'And the issue here is, if you have a shrinking group of younger people, who's going to look after the older people?

'The caring jobs are not particularly attractive – so who's going to do it?'

But as grim a realisation as that may be, maybe – just maybe – it's just what we need.

The Home Stretch

Over my many years as a business journalist, I've spoken to plenty of CEOs and senior executives in foreign multinationals – usually when they're wheeled out to talk up a new investment or expansion in their Irish operations. In these conversations the question 'Why Ireland?' invariably comes up – and in response, they tend to talk about the pool of talent here, the openness of the economy and the access it gives them to the European market. It's a carefully crafted answer – one that often skirts the importance of our low corporation tax – and it rarely strays from a very predictable script. That's because these executives tend to be media trained within an inch of their lives – and they like to keep anything even remotely controversial out of their public remarks. But there has been a subtle, but notable, change in their answers in recent years – they've started talking about housing.

It's usually pretty vague and broad stuff like: 'It is a challenge – but we have no problems finding the staff we need.'

'It's not affected us yet, but we're keeping an eye on it.'

This may sound somewhat tame to the untrained ear. But when you're used to hearing the usual ultra-sanitised PR speak that they traditionally stick to, this is almost like the equivalent of Alex Ferguson's hairdryer treatment. And clearly, it's a mounting problem for employers, big and small. Since 2022, surveys of US multinationals by the American Chamber of Commerce Ireland have consistently raised housing as one (if not the) key issue that needs to be addressed. Speaking at an Oireachtas Committee last year, ESRI research professor Kieran McQuinn said that multinationals with operations here saw housing as an area of 'significant concern'. A 2024 survey by Dublin Chamber found that two-thirds of companies had lost employees or potential recruits because of the housing crisis.

Ireland may indeed be an open economy with lots of talent and low taxes – but if the would-be workers can't afford to live here, or move closer to the jobs they're trained for, then our economic model, based on foreign direct investment, will find itself on rocky ground sooner rather than later.

And that's not to mention the fiscal challenges that the demographic changes will bring. As we've already seen, if our younger population are having less children while our older population are living longer, there will be a point at which the social welfare system comes under unbearable pressure. And it won't take until the Bailout Babies retire – it will happen a long time before that. Arguably, we're already seeing its effects.

Young people are traditionally the lifeblood of the hospitality and retail sectors – they work the low-paying jobs as a means to an end while they study for, and get a foothold in, their chosen career. But as there are fewer teens and early-twenty-somethings coming through the system, and wages have generally lagged behind the rising cost of living, so there are fewer people willing and able to do that kind of work. These sectors are important to the country's economy in and of themselves, and hospitality is a key cog in Ireland's wildly successful tourism industry too – but if there isn't the staff there to man the hotels, restaurants and cliché-riddled tours, then it could damage that revenue stream as well, and create a cascade effect on the country's coffers.

Worth bearing in mind next time you face a long queue for your latte.

The shrinking demographics and the reemergence of the Brain Drain can also be seen closer to home, given the growing number of tradespeople (like Joe from a previous chapter) heading abroad in order to earn the money they think they deserve. That goes some way towards explaining why the cost of getting so much as a light-switch rewired has gone through the roof. Somewhat ironically, it is also adding to the difficulty in ramping up housing supply across the country – with a lack of skilled trades acting as one of the bottlenecks in the construction system.

Meanwhile the country's care system – from hospitals to care homes to creches – is already under continuous staffing pressure, and heavily reliant on immigrant workers. As fewer young people come through the system, and fewer of them opt for what can be a challenging and poorly paying career, they will get even harder to staff – even more so given that an aging population will only add to demand for services. And, in the end, the likes of nursing homes will become even more expensive, putting more financial pressure on individuals, or the state, or both.

And if you have a shrinking workforce, leading to shrinking industries, then you end up with shrinking tax revenue. And the only way to address that is to cut spending or hike taxes on what's left – both of which would represent a shrinking of opportunity for people young and old. And potentially another reason to up sticks and find somewhere sunnier to live.

The hospitals will get even harder to staff, the nursing homes will get even more expensive and raising the amount needed for people's pensions will become too hard.

But maybe this is what it will take for things to change. One criticism that's repeatedly levied upon the current system is that it's designed to protect the haves rather than help the have-nots.

Landlords want to be able to keep charging as much rent as possible, developers don't want to see the value of their assets decline – even regular homeowners become vocal objectors to new homes being built if they think for a second that it will impact their property's value.

But the prospect of falling tax revenues, an unstable pensions scheme and a hollowed-out elderly care system probably isn't something they want to see either – even if it's just for entirely selfish reasons. Maybe it's this kind of existential threat to the entire economy – and the health and happiness of the 'haves' – that will force the country to have a real reckoning with the flaws in our housing system and all of the constituent parts that have forced many to put their futures on hold.

Potent potential

Another reason for optimism is the fact the Bailout Babies are a resilient, resourceful bunch.

Of course, there are some within the Bailout demographic who expect to get everything for nothing – or who have about as much financial restraint as Carrie Bradshaw. But, despite the tabloid stereotype that's often applied by default, it turns out that these are the outliers rather than the typical.

In their short lives they've seen, however briefly, a hint of the good life. Some of them might even have enjoyed a bit of it themselves. But for the most part, they've spent their time grappling with multiple financial crises, with a global pandemic thrown in for good measure. And as they now look toward their futures, they're seeing even the simple goal of building a life of their own continually slip further from their view – all while the world fractures, the climate changes and AI threatens to steal their job.

Given all of that, you'd understand if they made a collective decision to simply give up altogether – but they've not done that. Instead, they're trying everything they can to make their situation work for them. In the many conversations I've had with people in their 20s and 30s, I've heard frustration, anger and even resignation – but also determination, focus, savvy and good humour. As a generation, they are better educated than anyone who has come before; far from work-shy, they are actually working harder – in more complex jobs – and are finding new ways to earn on top of that. And they are willing to do the hard yards – saving what they can, sacrificing in many areas, all the while being more careful, considered and deliberate in their spending. They are more at ease with who they are – and more keen to acquire experiences rather than physical things. They are more aware of their impact on the planet – and are more mindful of their own health and the wellness of others, both mental and physical.

Really the worst thing you can say about them is that they're incredibly unlucky to have been born when they were. But if that luck can change, they could be a new golden generation.

And surely their luck has to change eventually, right? Or, maybe it's more likely that they'll just end up having to change it for themselves. After all, they are already reshaping everything from retail to pub culture and travel in their image. And they are a demographic in the ascendent – already accounting for more than a quarter of the country's adult population. They're even likely to find some kindred spirits in Gen Alpha who, barring a dramatic change, will be in the exact same predicament in the coming years. It may not be long until the Bailout Babies are in the majority.

I'm calling it now – Tinderman for Taoiseach.

Acknowledgements

My sincere thanks to everyone who spoke to me about their experiences, dreams, frustrations, and plans. This is your story – I hope I did it justice. Thanks too to the groups and businesses that allowed me to come along to their events and meet-ups to find the people who had stories to tell. Not to mention the experts and organisations that shared their knowledge with me, or helped me to navigate and gather the data that illustrates what the anecdotes suggest. A particular shout-out goes to John Byrne and the Central Statistics Office, who fielded more than a few oddly specific queries about their decades-spanning stats.

Thanks to everyone at Gill Books – especially Sarah, who saw the potential in a vague pitch, helped hone it into a fully fledged idea and offered a constant feed of advice, guidance and support that turned it into this book. Thanks to Isabelle for her support, feedback and tips – and for getting me back on track when my cultural references got too obscure (or too retro). Thanks too to Heidi and Emma for their edits and tweaks (and catching the odd typo…); and to Charlie and Graham for making it all look its best.

Thanks to all my colleagues in RTÉ News and Current Affairs; in particular the business desk crew. David, Petula, Glenda, Aengus, Gill, Brian, Gail and Fergal – who I'm lucky enough to count as colleagues – and special thanks to my former boss, Will. It's through my work with the *Today with Claire Byrne* programme that I've been able to take regular deep-dives on some of the more interesting, intangible and off-beat topics that can often get missed in the day-to-day of the news bulletins – one of which formed the spark of the idea for this book. So I am eternally grateful to Claire, Alastair and Niamh for giving me the opportunity to work with you, and always being open to my random pitches. And thanks to the rest of the *TwCB* team, past and present; namely Rachel, John, Ronan, Barbara, Nicole, Amy, Penny, Abie, Jarlath and Michelle. And to all of the other friends and colleagues in RTÉ who have been a sounding board, a support or a source of ideas (or all of the above). Specifically (but not limited) to Lynsey, Jackie, Samantha, Shane, Jackie, Evelyn, Áine, Laura W, Mary, George, Des, John, Laura F, Shay, Kate, Ailbhe, Karen, Audrey, Eleanor M, Brendan, Deirdre, Elayne, Eleanor B, Conor, Joan and Mick.

Thanks to Dave, Dan, Anto, Richie, John, Darren and Gerry – knowing there was always a Sunday pint on the go, along with a meandering chat about nothing and everything, kept me going on more than one occasion. Dave C – the quarterlies (and the supportive/insulting voice notes) were and are invaluable.

And last but most of all, thanks to my family.

Thanks to Iain and Amelia for the various ways they've supported me over the years; to Dad, Damien, Emily and Norah – and the wider Ward clan – for all the help they've given me. Thanks also to Mossey and Mary and Yseult – and specifically Tomás and Sarah for the loan of the desk space.

Thanks to Fiadh and Ruadhán for the vital daily distraction (and the even more important hugs).

My endless thanks and love to my Mam, who gave me my curiosity and a willingness to give things a try. You always encouraged me to do what I loved – and did everything in your power to make sure I could. None of this would exist if it wasn't for you.

And to Sarah. You made it possible for me to devote the time and effort required to work on this project without a second of hesitation, cheered me on and kept me going every step of the way. But – more than that – your constant love, support and belief in me has been the source (and cause) of everything good in my life. I am lucky beyond words.